Confidence
Unleashed

To my daughter,
may she rule the world.

First Edition

ISBN 978-1-66-295598-3 (paperback)
ISBN 978-1-66-295599-0 (ebook)

Designed by Liliana Guia
Edited by Corrie Jackson
Illustrations by naqiewei/iStockphoto; IssaraJarukitjaroon/iStockphoto (Challenges)

Published in the United States by Gatekeeper Press

Confidence Unleashed

10 Kick-Ass Strategies to *Grow* as a Leader

(WITHOUT CHANGING WHO YOU ARE)

INSPIRED BY A DECADE
OF MENTORING YOUNG WOMEN

Sheri West

Confidence Unleashed

"I don't know what the future holds, but I know who holds the future."

—OPRAH

Picture this: It's the late 1990s. I have big hair, shoulder pads, and bright red lipstick. I have recently graduated from Michigan State University with a Masters in Leadership Development. With an internship at PepsiCo under my belt, I am ready to conquer the corporate world at GE.

Except I don't. It takes me much longer than anticipated to learn the "unwritten rules" and navigate office politics. I learn the hard way that perception is key—how you dress, communicate, and present yourself profoundly impacts your path. I am often the only woman in the room. I don't have access to mentors or sponsors that look like me.

I work hard. I rise up the corporate ladder. But I struggle with building the right strategic relationships through networking, which often comes easily for men—relationships frequently strengthened by a round of golf. I wrestle with achieving the right balance between being assertive and not coming across as overly aggressive. The double bind for women in leadership is real: being perceived as either too soft or too harsh. These challenges shape my journey and fuel my determination to support other women.

After nearly two decades in Corporate America, I decide to live the mantra "lift as we climb" and in 2014 create LiveGirl, a women's leadership organization dedicated to paying it forward to the next generation. My mission: to share the "unwritten rules" and equip young women with the mentors, skills, and experiences necessary to become confident, inclusive leaders and thrive.

Over a decade, we serve nearly 18,000 girls, changing lives as we go. I want to do more. So, I decide to turn the invaluable lessons I learned mentoring young women into a kick-ass workbook.

Why is this so important to me? For starters, I am the proud mother of a brilliant college-aged daughter who will soon launch into the workforce. So, it's personal. Because when I think back to my Corporate America experience, *I wouldn't want my daughter to work there.* I am deeply committed to doing whatever I can to build a more equal, inclusive future for my daughter—and for everyone. I hope this workbook gives more young women access to the crucial lessons that will accelerate their careers and help drive gender parity.

You see, girls' confidence plummets during adolescence and usually never fully recovers. In the workforce, women are still underrepresented in leadership and positions of power. Despite being half of the workforce, women comprise only 10% of Fortune 500 CEOs—and there are only two Black women CEOs. A recent report showed that, for the first time in two decades, the number of women in leadership is actually declining.[1]

We've long talked about the "glass ceiling" in senior leadership, but we must focus on the **start** of a woman's career to truly overcome disparities. The biggest obstacle women face on the path to leadership is the **very first step up** to manager, called the **"broken rung"**. For every 100 men promoted and hired to manager, only 72 women are promoted and hired. And it's worse for women of color. This early inequality has a long-term impact on career advancement.[2]

How will this book help? While acknowledging damaging biases and systemic barriers, especially for women of color, this workbook focuses on aspects *within your control* to build your leadership skills and career confidence. This book aims to equip you with the mindset and skills to thrive in the rapidly evolving workplace and mend that broken rung.

After all, leadership is not top-down but all-around. Whether you are just starting in your career or are in a position of power, we all have a role to play. Leadership is about influence, initiative, drive, and impact—regardless of your position in an organizational structure. This book will help you **lead yourself** so that you can rise and lead others.

So, let's get started...

HOW TO USE THIS BOOK

Inspired by a decade of mentoring young women (like you), I have synthesized relevant, helpful research and provided evidence-based strategies to employ. Think of it as your mentorship guidebook—or a leadership operating manual.

I have structured the book across two sections, intentionally designed with a floral motif. Think of Part I (Shift Your Mindset) as preparing the soil and planting the seeds, and Part II (Build Your Skills) as tending your plants so that they bloom into flowers (not weeds!). Put together, through a series of challenges, you will learn how to shift your mindset, build your skills, and become the leader you were meant to be.

I have woven in personal stories and crafted fun, engaging exercises (some are even choose-your-own adventures!). Go at your own pace—it doesn't matter if you complete the workbook in one week, one month, or one year. I encourage you to take time to reflect on the material and prompts. It might be tempting to just think about the questions rather than write them out, but writing requires deeper thinking and will provide you with more impactful results. As you know, you get out what you put in—and according to the National Training Laboratories, you only remember 10% of what you read, but 90% of what you *do*.

Also, I intended for you to work from front to back, but you may skip around if that makes your heart sing! But promise me, no matter what, you will say the affirmation at the end of each chapter aloud. Manifest your voice in this world. Finally, I encourage you to enlist an accountability partner. Engage a mentor, friend, or parent—someone with whom you may debrief and process your findings and revelations.

Remember, I believe in you. If you put in the work, this book will help you develop both the mindset and skills needed to unleash your confidence and help you grow into the leader you were born to be. My goal is that, by the end, you will clearly see that **the power is inside of you; the power to shape your future is ready to be unleashed.**

You are a marvel. Keep shining.

Sheri West

Sheri@Confidence-Unleashed.com
#ConfidenceUnleashed

PART I

Shift
mind

your
set

01.
own your journey

"Start by knowing who you are and what you want, build credibility around it, and deliver it compellingly."

—KRISTA NEHER, CEO & AUTHOR

Begin by defining your personal brand. This is your story, no one else's.

Here we go! The first step on your path to unlocking your leadership potential, and building a successful career, is to own your journey. This means taking ownership of your experiences, successes, failures, and the path you have followed (and continue to pursue). So, let's embrace your story, learn from it, and use it to shape your future. We will start with your personal brand, which embodies your unique value proposition. It is crucial to establish your identity and take control of your narrative. By intentionally shaping how you present yourself to the world *from the outset*, you will 'hang a guiding star' for your career leadership journey.

This chapter will guide you through three key steps to creating an authentic, compelling personal brand:

1. *Identify Your Unique Selling Point (USP)*
2. *Shape Your Narrative*
3. *Refine Your Personal Brand*

A strong personal brand will increase your credibility and help you stand apart. Ready? Let's go!

71%

of professionals say a good personal brand opens the door to new career opportunities[3]

WHAT IS A PERSONAL BRAND?

If I mention Nike, Dove, or Coca-Cola, what immediately springs to mind? Chances are, you already have a clear perception of what these brands represent, as they are consistently regarded as the 'most authentic brands' by Gen Z.[4] Just like these companies, *you* have a personal brand, and this brand's job is to identify **who you are with clarity, authenticity, and consistency.** As my mentee, Molly, aptly says, "You can't figure out where you want to go in life if you're not connected with your mind." Excellent point!

It is important to recognize that first impressions are formed rapidly, and can significantly influence subsequent interactions and perceptions. Did you know that people assess whether you're likable, trustworthy, and competent *within the first seven seconds* of meeting you?

How you present yourself—through wardrobe, body language, social media, and communications—contributes to your personal brand, and greatly influences how people respond to you. So take control! Be intentional about cultivating your personal brand and shaping your narrative. If you don't define who you are, people will likely make assumptions, perhaps incorrectly. Your personal brand should reflect your values, strengths, aspirations, and *who you truly are*. Authenticity is key.

Growing up on a farm in Portland, Michigan, I never dreamed that I would land in Corporate America. My mom was a teacher and my dad was an electrician—they couldn't offer guidance into the world of suits, boardrooms, and high-rise buildings. It was a journey that began with uncertainty but promised opportunity.

My first taste of the corporate world came via an internship at PepsiCo. Walking into the bustling headquarters, I felt both excited and overwhelmed by the sheer scale of it. As I navigated the cubicles and conference rooms, I quickly realized that I had entered a realm where personal branding was paramount. However, personal branding was a concept that eluded me at the time. Raised in a close-knit community where reputation was built on character and integrity, the idea of crafting a persona seemed foreign and, perhaps, a tad superficial. As I observed my colleagues effortlessly handle social interactions and professional networks, however, I began to see that personal branding was more than just a buzzword—it was a necessity to achieve success in the arena.

So, I embraced the opportunity to learn and adapt. I observed the way that seasoned professionals approached boardroom conversations, curated their online profiles, crafted compelling narratives, and cultivated meaningful connections. I learned that personal branding was not about fabricating an image, but about **authentically showcasing one's values, experiences, and aspirations.** No matter where we come from, we can shape our own narrative and define our own success.

So, let's start building your personal brand! Here are three steps that will create a compelling narrative that gets you noticed and drives you forward.

Step 1:
Identify Your Unique Selling Point (USP)

Your Unique Selling Point (USP) encapsulates the distinct qualities, skills, experiences, or attributes that set you apart from others. It highlights what makes you uniquely valuable and forms the basis of your personal brand.

Early in my career, I was uncertain whether I possessed a USP. Surrounded by co-workers with more experience and fancy degrees, how was it possible that I could add unique value? I have come to understand that everyone possesses unique strengths, skills, and experiences that contribute value in different ways. Upon graduation, I started my career at GE, with my first assignment at a GE Electrical Distribution & Control manufacturing facility. There, I learned that my approachable, upbeat, and inclusive nature resonated well with the factory workers. They were soon approaching *me* (the newbie!) with ideas.

Trust me, your USP will serve as the building block of your personal brand. As Oscar Wilde said, "Be yourself; everyone else is already taken." The first step towards identifying your USP is to craft a vision statement. So, let's dive into the first challenge.

Challenge

Create Your Personal Brand Vision Statement

I remember early in my career at GE, my human resources manager challenged me to reflect upon my personal brand and describe myself in three words. I stumbled through three words but couldn't fully connect them to myself. Since then, I have revisited this question often, letting the answer guide me. Today, if you were to ask, **I would describe myself as a *tenacious*, *inclusive*, and *innovative* leader.** I operate with intention—whether accepting speaking engagements, posting on LinkedIn, or meeting new people—to ensure I am aligned with these core values.

Now, let's identify yours. Start by selecting three power adjectives from the list below (or come up with your own).

I am _____

Adaptable	Empathetic	Proactive
Ambitious	Empowering	Reliable
Authentic	Enthusiastic	Resilient
Charismatic	Influential	Resourceful
Collaborative	Innovative	Solution-Oriented
Confident	Insightful	Strategic
Creative	Inclusive	Tenacious
Determined	Motivated	Versatile
Dynamic	Passionate	Visionary

Now, let's define what you bring to the table. Identify the core values and strengths that set you apart. If you get stuck, think of a recent accomplishment (or challenge you overcame) that made you proud—and identify the values and strengths that made the accomplishment possible. For example, it could be a successful project implementation (finally! Salesforce is in!), or it could be that time you received a tough email, clearly conveying a miscommunication, that you resolved with the sender. Still stuck? Reach out to a friend, family member, or mentor and ask for their input on your strengths and unique qualities. Sometimes, others can offer valuable insights and perspectives that you may not have considered.

Identify your most important strengths, values, and career/ leadership aspirations.

_____

_____

_____

_____

_____

_____

_____

_____

_____

_____

_____

Now, take a moment to study the result and craft your vision statement reflecting your power adjectives, strengths, values, and career aspirations.

Here is my example:

"I am an inclusive, innovative social impact leader, and I am on a mission to make the world a better place."

My personal brand vision statement:

_____

_____

_____

_____

_____

_____

_____

_____

_____

"When we know our value and can express our value, we're able to teach others how to honour what we bring to the table."

—CLEO WADE, WRITER & ARTIST

Decode the Dress Code

First impressions matter for your personal brand, and what you wear plays a significant role in shaping that initial impression. I always recommend that you 'dress to impress', and seek ways to balance personal style with professional attire that meets workplace standards. I've received numerous inquiries from mentees about tattoos and piercings and, while they are forms of self-expression, it is vital to recognize that some work cultures may not embrace them. Therefore, understanding your professional environment's expectations and norms is essential. Thoughtfully selecting attire that aligns with these expectations not only communicates professionalism but also showcases adaptability and respect for workplace standards. Meaghan, a mentee, sought my advice on this matter. She had been offered an internship at a bank that prohibited visible piercings, which she was unwilling to remove. I advised her to approach the human resources manager respectfully and inquire whether there was flexibility in this aspect of the dress code.* In this instance, the HR manager responded that a nose piercing was fine. However, if a professional dress code clashes with your values and lacks flexibility, it's perfectly acceptable to conclude that the environment may not be suitable for you. At the end of the day, wear what makes you happy, and more importantly, what represents your brand.

*TRY THIS: *"While I understand and respect the company's dress code policy, I wanted to ask if there is any flexibility (with X) that could accommodate my personal values without compromising my professionalism."*

Step 2:
Shape Your Narrative

Now that you have identified your USP and defined your vision statement, it is time to begin shaping your narrative. Let's start with your 'elevator pitch.' What does this mean? An elevator pitch is a brief (think 30-60 seconds!) speech that highlights your strengths, accomplishments, and passions concisely and compellingly. I learned this lesson the hard way when, during my first assignment at GE corporate, I crossed paths with then-CEO, Jack Welch. As I followed my manager into a meeting, Jack noticed me and said, "Who are you?" I recited my name and title. "No!" Jack thundered. "Sell me! Give me your elevator pitch!"

Recently, I asked Shaindy, one of my mentees, to describe herself. "I guess I would say that I am pretty smart and usually resilient," Shaindy told me. I wanted to jump out of my seat and shout (like Jack had at me), "That's not all! Don't sell yourself short!"

To be clear, describing yourself with positive and powerful adjectives is not bragging; it's an essential step in establishing a powerful personal brand. **Be bold and assertive, and don't fall into the trap of holding yourself back from affirming your worth.** If necessary, 'unlearn' the societal girlhood commandment of humility and modesty. (Need inspiration? Look at how Taylor Swift affirmed her worth by reclaiming ownership of her master recordings. She demonstrated confidence in her worth and the value of her creative work. Be like Taylor. Live your *Confident Era*.) You WILL be asked by a hiring manager, colleague, or new contact to 'describe yourself.' What they really mean is, 'pitch yourself.' So, what will you say?

Challenge

Craft Your Elevator Pitch

It's not easy to describe yourself, your strengths, your accomplishments, plus your "ask" in a couple of sentences. That is why you need to thoughtfully craft—and practice—your pitch. Trust me, having an intentional elevator pitch is worth the investment and will set you apart from the competition. It certainly beats that horrifying moment of stumbling through a muddled answer. Guaranteed, you will find yourself using your elevator pitch often.

Craft a 30-60 second pitch with the following elements:
    [Who you are]
    [What you do and why you're passionate about it]
    [Your USP]
    [Your "ask" or conclusion—tailor to audience]

Job Seekers (Early Career) Example:
    "Hello! My name is Asija. I am excited to graduate cum laude with a degree in Government/International Affairs this May. My extensive work experience and family heritage have instilled in me a passion for international public policy. I am global-minded, strategic, and inquisitive. I would love to schedule a networking meeting to explore opportunities at your company."

Career Climbers (Breaking The Glass Ceiling) Example:

"Hello! I am Sheri West, a Founder and CEO, champion of equity and inclusion, and former management executive turned social entrepreneur with over 25 years of corporate and leadership development experience. A decade ago, I founded LiveGirl to pay it forward to the next generation of diverse female leaders. I am passionate about gender parity and inclusion, and would love to explore opportunities for us to make an impact together."

Now, it's your turn. After drafting your pitch, practice it out loud. (You know the saying, practice makes perfect!) Time yourself and enlist a friend to listen and provide feedback. Keep tweaking until you feel confident!

My elevator pitch:

_____

_____

_____

_____

_____

_____

_____

_____

_____

_____

_____

BE AUTHENTIC

The best way to shape your narrative, and own your brand, is to be authentic and embrace who you are. I am proud of the fact that when people think of me they *know* how passionate I am about women's leadership and inclusion. It's true, I have been told that I am 'too much' for some people. However, I do not let this fact deter me from being true to my brand and my values. As my favorite poet, Mary Oliver, says, "Let me always be who I am, and then some." I am confident that I will come to mind when opportunities relating to equity and inclusion arise, which is my goal. Authenticity builds trust and credibility with your audience.

"Owning who we are is power. We've got to dare to stand out."

—JANET MOCK, AUTHOR & TRANSGENDER RIGHTS ACTIVIST

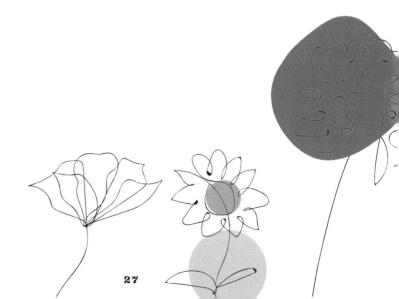

Sharing Your Pronouns

————

Sharing more of your identity, including your pronouns, may be an important part of your brand. Embracing inclusivity and respecting diverse gender identities not only fosters a welcoming environment, but also showcases a commitment to equity and understanding within the workplace. Companies have made significant strides in advancing LGBTQ+ equal protections and benefits. Increasing numbers of people are embracing their authentic identities in the workplace, and are being accepted for doing so.

Of course, prejudice and discrimination still exist, and have the potential to create a toxic work environment. That being said, there is an *upside*: openly discussing an important aspect of your identity can also lead to affirming experiences, such as support from colleagues, as well as encouraging others to embrace their authentic selves, too. According to a recent *Harvard Business Review* report,[5] "an emerging body of research suggests that being open and authentic about one's invisible identities typically yields positive psychological and job outcomes." Ultimately, you should share your pronouns if they are important to you, and seek out a work environment that celebrates your identity.

"Speaking as a non-cisgender person, it can be difficult to communicate your identity and pronouns in the workplace—and this is especially true when you're the only one doing so. But to be authentic, you have to share who you really are. The best advice I can give is to only work in spaces where your differences are celebrated."
—Han, Mentee

Step 3:
Refine Your
Personal Brand

You have identified your USP and shaped your narrative (well done!), so now it's time to move on to the final step: refining your personal brand. It's not enough to do Steps 1 and 2 and leave it there. It is crucial to maintain consistency across all facets of your personal brand, including (especially!) social media. Your online presence is an essential part of your personal brand, influencing how both current and potential colleagues and managers perceive you. You must assume that a hiring manager will Google you and/or review your social media accounts. You may be the best candidate for a position, but an unprofessional social media account, inconsistent with your brand, could cost you opportunities. (That is why I encourage you to keep your personal social media accounts private.) It is vital to ensure consistent alignment with your brand across all platforms.

Challenge

Perform A Personal Brand Audit

In this exercise, you'll use a critical eye to review your branding assets, and evaluate your digital footprint across all social media platforms and professional networks to ensure consistency.

1. **Make a list of all the online platforms where you have a public account,** including social media platforms (such as LinkedIn, X, Facebook, and Instagram), professional networking sites, personal websites or blogs, and any other online forums or communities where you engage.

_____

_____

_____

_____

_____

_____

_____

_____

2. **Review your profile picture, bio, work experience, education, skills, and any other relevant sections.**

3. **Ensure consistency across all your online platforms** in terms of profile information, branding elements, messaging, and tone of voice. Consistency helps reinforce your personal brand and makes a stronger impression on your audience.

4. **Finally, Google yourself and review what a potential employer may see.** If you find unprofessional images that are potentially harmful, reach out to the account owners and politely request their removal. If necessary, consider seeking assistance from online reputation management professionals who specialize in managing and improving individuals' online presence.

My Brand Audit:

_____

_____

_____

_____

_____

_____

_____

_____

Notes & Actions:

_____

_____

_____

_____

_____

_____

_____

_____

Complete this audit to ensure that your online presence aligns with your personal brand and presents a consistent, professional image.

Rock your Resume

Early in your career, your resume will be your most important personal branding asset. So, listen up! According to research, recruiters spend an average of only *six to eight seconds* reading a resume. That's not a lot of time! Therefore, invest time and "polish" it. Be sure that your resume effectively conveys your objectives, strengths, and key selling points.

I review hundreds of resumes annually, and here are my top "must-do" resume tips:

1. Highlight your **skills**! According to Glassdoor, 67% of hiring managers spend the most time reviewing the **experience** section.[6] They are looking for <u>transferable</u> skills. 90% look for evidence of 'problem-solving' and 80% look for 'teamwork' skills. If you are an early career job seeker, you may be thinking, "But I don't yet have much experience!" Yes, you do! Leverage relevant coursework, clubs, activities, honors, awards, scholarships, etc. to highlight transferable skills.

2. Proofread multiple times! Seek feedback and meticulously check for grammar and spelling errors. Ask a friend to proofread your resume. Use grammar-checking software!

3. Upload your resume to LinkedIn. Your resume information can be utilized to personalize your feed and suggest relevant job opportunities. This step also enhances the likelihood of recruiters or hiring managers discovering your profile. Additionally, you'll receive tailored LinkedIn Learning course suggestions to further develop your skills. All in all, it's a win-win situation!

EVOLVE YOUR PERSONAL BRAND

It is important to note that as you grow, your personal brand will grow too. As you evolve, aspects of your personal brand may no longer align. For instance, I needed to shed certain aspects of my corporate persona to fully develop into a social impact leader. Personal growth often requires you to edit your identity to grow past it. It is important to revisit your personal brand regularly, assess its clarity, authenticity, and consistency, and adapt as needed.

Having a clear, authentic, and consistent personal brand makes it easier for employers and others to recognize your value-add. When this is in place, you will "shine bright like a diamond," as Rihanna says. A strong personal brand will help you achieve your goals and build a successful career.

AFFIRMATION

"I have unique talents and deserve a seat at the table."

Identify what makes you uniquely valuable & what you bring to the table

———

Own who you are & authentically shape your narrative

———

Maintain consistency across all facets of your personal brand

02.
know your purpose

"Your purpose is your 'why'–it's the reason you get out of bed every morning and the driving force behind everything you do."

—MELINDA GATES, HUMANITARIAN

Blaze a unique trail and don't let the expectations of others limit you.

Onward! It's time to cast off the expectations of who others think you **should be** and define **who you aspire to become**. Discovering your professional purpose involves uncovering what truly ignites your passion, allowing you to align your career with your core values. This is important because research shows that when you are passionate about your work, you're much more likely to thrive. Considering that, on average, individuals spend about 90,000 hours (or one-third) of their lives working,[7] wouldn't you prefer to feel purposefully aligned in your pursuits?

This chapter will guide you through three key steps to help you identify your purpose, allowing you to blaze your trail in the right direction:

1. *Discover Your Why*
2. *Pin Down Your Professional Purpose*
3. *Map Your Journey*

When you understand your purpose, you can align your actions, goals, and decisions with what truly matters to you.

5.5

the number of
times more likely
that employees
aligned with their
purpose experience
higher levels of
well-being and
job satisfaction[8]

I grew up in a small farming community where I didn't have a clear sense of my professional purpose. Beyond my mom and aunts, who were teachers, I had a limited view of my professional options. When I entered college, I aspired to be a TV news reporter (I remember interviewing family members, pretending to be Barbara Walters!). Later, frustrated and unsure of my direction, I changed my major several times. Then, a career counselor offered a perspective shift, suggesting that I was fixating too much on **what** I wanted to be rather than **who** I wanted to be. Aha! This was a groundbreaking perspective for me.

Focusing on the "who", rather than the "what", made me realize that I wanted to launch my career in the business realm, and establish a strong foundation of leadership skills. This way, I could make a meaningful impact regardless of where my journey took me.

Many of us, especially those without early access to mentors, struggle with defining our purpose early on. I have had too many conversations with mentees that go like this:

Me: What kind of career path are you considering?

Mentee: I'm aiming for something in X.

Me: Why X?

Mentee: Well, my parents mentioned it, and it seems likely to lead to good job opportunities.

Me: Does X align with your professional purpose?

Mentee: I'm not sure!

This is what I tell my mentees: instead of dwelling on the "what" (such as a specific job title), focus on *who you want to be*. Don't tether yourself to societal or parental expectations, nor limit yourself to the possibilities already known. (Perhaps you will even create your own job, like I did as a social entrepreneur!)

Also, I want to clarify that you don't have to know exactly where you want to end up in 20 or 30 years. (Whew! The world is changing so fast, we can't even predict what jobs will exist then!) But defining your purpose is essential in order to provide guidance, and clarity, and inform your direction. Remember, **your direction is more important than your speed.** If you're racing at 100 MPH in the wrong direction, you won't get any closer to your real goal!

With that in mind, here are three steps to ensure you're heading in the right direction.

Step 1:
Discover Your Why

The author Simon Sinek said, "When you have a clear why, the what becomes flexible." I've discovered that when I stay focused on my why—and feel aligned with my values and how I invest my time—I'm illuminated from the inside out. I shine brighter.

In a world of constant change and loud (!), competing voices, understanding your *why*—your mission, calling, and purpose—is essential. Remember, this is **your** journey (not your parents' or anyone else's). To step into your power, you must understand what makes you *tick*. Confidence is built by trusting yourself, which you can only do—in my mind—if you have a plan. So, the idea is to make a plan, using your *why* as the guiding force behind your actions and decisions, to help steer your career journey.

Challenge

Define + Align Your *Why*

Part 1: *Define*. First, let's take a moment to reflect. So, either a) Put on a cowboy hat and crank up Beyoncé OR b) Find some quiet "me time" and answer the following questions:

1. **What excites me and makes me feel alive, useful, and engaged?**
2. **If money were no object, what would I choose to do for work?**
3. **What would my life look like if I boldly stepped into the best version of myself?**

Write down your thoughts, feelings, and insights. Be honest! Don't filter your thoughts.

Define:

_____

_____

_____

_____

_____

_____

_____

_____

_____

_____

Part 2: *Align.* Now, let's use a **Why Venn Diagram** to identify the sweet spot at the intersection of these three variables: *what you're good at, what brings you joy, and what work needs doing.*

What happens when you don't align your career with your *why*? You end up "floating"—aka lacking clear intention or direction, and floating along a career path, or from job to job. This happened to my mentee, Jess, who had landed in a corporate marketing role. While Jess loved marketing, and specifically graphic design, she did not love her area of responsibility—designing corporate presentations and annual reports. She was floating. Here is how Jess used the **Why Venn Diagram** to analyze her career alignment:

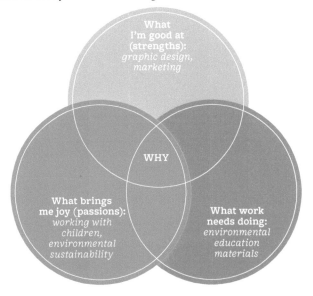

Jess concluded that she wanted to explore marketing in different sectors. She tapped her mentor (me!), leveraged her personal board of directors (more on this later), and worked on cultivating the mindset needed to pivot with confidence and forge a new path for herself. Ultimately, she applied for various positions and landed a marketing role at EcoRise, which proved to be a perfect fit.

Similarly, a decade ago, I undertook this exercise, which prompted my pivot from Corporate America to the nonprofit sector. Take a look:

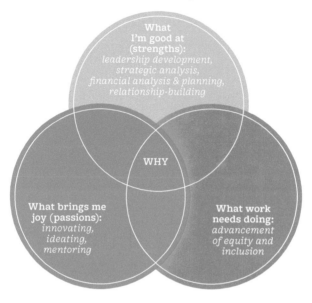

My *Why* answer = Establish a nonprofit focused on young women's leadership and gender parity. Now it's your turn!

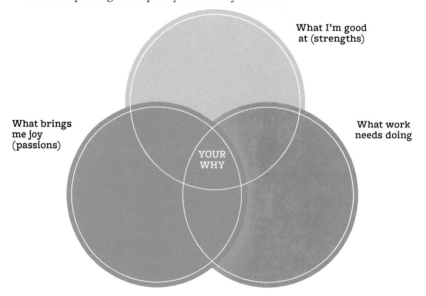

Step 2: Pin Down Your Professional Purpose

Now it's time to craft a professional purpose statement that resonates with your *why* and values. Your values are the **core principles and beliefs** that drive your decisions and actions. They should serve as guiding lights as you navigate your professional journey. Your purpose statement should encapsulate what you feel deeply compelled to achieve in life. It will serve as both your moral and career compass, guiding you through uncertain and challenging times.

Note that there are no right or wrong answers here. I've learned that successful leaders prioritize leading with their values. Ultimately, leaders aligned with their 'why' and values exude unparalleled confidence.

Challenge

Identify Your Values + Professional Impact

Read the list below and circle the ten values that most resonate with you. From this list, identify the five that are most important.

Acceptance	Equality	Optimism
Accomplishment	Faith	Peace
Achievement	Fame	Power
Adaptability	Family happiness	Recognition
Adventure	Financial security	Reliability
Affection	Flexibility	Religion
Affiliation	Freedom	Resilience
Ambition	Gratitude	Respect
Authenticity	Grit	Responsibility
Authority	Growth	Self-Awareness
Beauty	Happiness	Self-Respect
Belonging	Health	Social Impact
Challenge	Honesty	Spirituality
Compassion	Hope	Success
Competence	Impact	Sustainability
Control	Inclusivity	Teamwork
Courage	Independence	Thoughtfulness
Creativity	Innovation	Timeliness
Community	Integrity	Tradition
Curiosity	Joy	Transparency
Connection	Learning	Vision
Dependability	Loyalty	Wealth
Discovery	Love	Wisdom
Education	Mindfulness	Wonder
Empathy	Nature	_____
		Or write in your own

Now write 2-3 sentences summarizing how you will connect your *why* and values to make a professional impact.

My Values:

Compassion, Innovation, Social Impact

My Professional Purpose Statement:

I am committed to harnessing my gratitude, passion for equity and inclusion, and compassion to pay it forward and serve women and girls. Through innovative approaches and strategic partnerships, I will leverage my strengths to create meaningful and sustainable social impact.

Now it's your turn!

My Values:

_____

_____

_____

_____

My Professional Purpose Statement:

_____

_____

_____

_____

_____

_____

EMBRACE WHO YOU ARE BECOMING

CAREER MYTH: *There is a dream job for everyone.*
FACT CHECK: *You will learn from all experiences, and there is no single, be-all-end-all "dream" job.*

Your early career will be filled with discovery; every job has its ups and downs. (In other words, it's not all sunshine and rainbows!) I often see young women holding out for an elusive "dream" job, missing out on valuable opportunities in the meantime. Does a dream job even exist? Many people assume that I have a dream job as the founder of my own company. However, while I *do* mostly love my job—formulating strategies, building partnerships, and coaching young women—there are aspects I don't enjoy as much, like fundraising and tight budgets.

The objective, then, is to secure positions that resonate with your professional purpose, allowing you to learn, contribute, and grow, even if they don't constitute your ultimate dream job. Along the way, you'll gain valuable insights about yourself, which will inform your future career endeavors and personal growth. This journey is a lifelong evolution. You might even undergo a complete transformation, as my mentee, Kira, did. Kira realized that she wasn't fulfilling her professional purpose through her lucrative Wall Street job, and so she left to attend medical school. (Many thought she was crazy! But I can assure you that she is very happy, indeed.) Keep in mind, your professional purpose isn't solely about the work you do; it's also about **who you are becoming** along the way.

"For me, becoming isn't about arriving somewhere or achieving a certain aim. I see it instead as forward motion, a means of evolving, a way to reach continuously toward a better self. The journey doesn't end."

—MICHELLE OBAMA

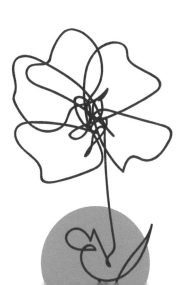

Step 3:
Map Your Journey

Now you are on your way! The next step is to activate your professional purpose by identifying your goals and implementation intentions. The key to progress lies in clearly defining the *what, how,* and *when.* Here are my proven "get stuff done" tips:

1. Set **SMART** goals: Specific - Measurable - Achievable - Relevant - Time-bound

2. Set **Implementation Intentions:** phrases that specify the **action, time,** and **location** for how you will "get stuff done". I promise that the specificity will improve your execution!

I also encourage you to enlist what I call a "progress pal" to set you up for success.

Regrettably, it's often the case that we're more inclined to disappoint ourselves than others. Research shows that individuals who share their goals with someone else tend to be more committed to their goals and more likely to achieve them. A progress pal can be a trusted friend, colleague, mentor, or coach who understands your objectives and is committed to helping you achieve them. She can help you stay focused on your goals by providing support, encouragement, and accountability. The key is to schedule ongoing meetings with your progress pal.

P.S. I want to give a shout-out to Fran Hauser, who served as my progress pal when I was writing this book!

95%

of us are
more likely to
achieve a goal
when we share it
and regularly
'check in' with
another person'

Challenge

Commit to Goals & Implementation Intentions

Ready to activate and blaze your trail?! (Give your trail a fun name! I call mine "Adventure Avenue"!) You must set both short-term and long-term goals to get there. By reflecting on the skills, experiences, and achievements you want to acquire in the next 12-18 months, and envisioning your desired future, you will gain insight into your professional direction. You will then set implementation intentions and enlist a progress pal to foster accountability and ensure success.

1. **My trail name:** Be creative!

   _____

   _____

2. **What skills, experiences, or achievements do I want to gain in the next 12-18 months?** What are your skill and experience gaps? Look for job postings in your field or specific roles you're interested in. Analyze the skills and qualifications that employers list as requirements or preferences. You can also utilize LinkedIn's job insights feature to explore the skills that are in demand for specific roles or industries. This tool provides valuable data on the skills that are most commonly listed in job postings.

   _____

   _____

   _____

   _____

3. **What are my short-term goals?** Identify short-term goals to address the gaps identified above. This could include securing an experienceship, internship, or entry-level position in your desired industry; networking with professionals; and/or completing a relevant course or training certification program. Be sure to set realistic and achievable goals.

_____

_____

_____

_____

4. **What are some of my long-term goals? If I could wave a magic wand, what would my life look like in 5 years?** Imagine where you see yourself in the long term, whether it's five years, ten years, or even further down the road. Define your long-term goals in clear and specific terms. For example, instead of saying "I want to be successful," specify what success means to you and how you will measure it. Long-term goals might involve advancing to a managerial position, specializing in a particular area, starting your own business, or writing a book!

_____

_____

_____

_____

_____

_____

5. **What is my Implementation Intention?** Complete this sentence:

"I will _____ *at* _____ *in* _____*."*

       [behavior]   *[time]*   *[location]*

6. **Who will be my progress pal?** Think of a mentor, colleague, or friend who can provide support, guidance, and accountability as you progress toward your goals. Remember, you'll need to regularly review and adjust your goals with your progress pal.

_____

_____

_____

_____

_____

_____

7. **My Commitment: I commit to reaching out to my designated progress pal by:**

_____

Date

_____

[Sign here]

Say Yes to Career Discovery

Part of owning your journey is to really put yourself out there and explore the many different possible career paths that align with your professional purpose. It is important to seek out opportunities to gain exposure to diverse experiences and perspectives. This may involve internships, professional networking events, volunteer work, informational interviews, job shadowing, or participating in extracurricular activities that allow you to discover your unique talents and joys. Say YES! to these opportunities as they arise. I bet you will find that you acquire more transferable knowledge and skills through experiences outside of the classroom. They will likely foster critical thinking, problem-solving, communication skills, and emotional intelligence, which are highly valued by employers and essential for success in any career path.

Repeat

**Gain
Self-Knowledge**
*(align why, values,
professional impact)*

Take Heart!
(you are making progress)

**CAREER
DISCOVERY**

Explore
*(majors, careers,
internships, experiences)*

Reflect
(focus your path)

Have Fun!
(try things out)

EMBRACE THE TWISTS AND TURNS

CAREER MYTH: *Careers follow a linear path to success.*
FACT CHECK: *There are numerous paths you can pursue to realize your professional purpose.*

It's time to debunk another career myth! Many of us have been conditioned to believe that there's only one clear route to success. However, in our dynamic world, this notion doesn't hold true. Sheryl Sandberg, founder of the global women's leadership community, Lean In, wisely observed, "A real career is not a ladder but a zigzagging, unpredictable path." According to the Bureau of Labor Statistics, the average person will have 12 different jobs in their career. So, expect a lot of changes along the way! Personally, my career has been a series of diverse chapters, moving from the for-profit to the nonprofit sector. Through it all, I've learned to embrace the twists and turns while staying true to my *why*. Remain open to new opportunities, challenges, and experiences that can foster both professional and personal growth.

Success   Success

what people think   what it really
it looks like   looks like

"People who repeatedly find career success learn to broaden their perspective and understand that there are always several roads to getting where you want to go."

—CARLA HARRIS, BUSINESS EXECUTIVE & BESTSELLING AUTHOR OF *LEAD TO WIN*

Try this: If you tend to feel anxious due to unknowns or changes in plan, try keeping a *Change Reflection Journal,* where you document instances of change in your life. For each change, reflect on how it brought new opportunities, learning experiences, or unexpected positive outcomes. You will soon gain confidence in knowing that you can embrace and benefit from change!

Since launching the *Confident* podcast with my college-aged daughter four years ago, we've had the privilege of interviewing hundreds of accomplished women, delving into the intricacies of their career paths and personal stories. A common thread across these episodes? The many twists and turns these accomplished women have navigated— sometimes even taking a step back to ultimately move forward.

Take Christine Laperriere, for example. Initially trained as an automotive design engineer, she transitioned to become the founder of a leadership development organization. After a decade as an engineer, she discovered her true passion lay in solving problems, which she now applies to people rather than cars.

Then there's Derby Chukwudi, a financial analyst at JPMorgan Chase, who decided to pursue her dream of competing for Miss New Jersey—and won! Notably, she became the first Nigerian American and Wall Street professional to hold the title.

Finally, my best friend, Karen McDonald's, journey is equally inspiring. She began her career as a high-school English teacher, then made a significant shift. She attended law school, qualified as a family court lawyer, then judge, and is now a prosecutor in Michigan. Google her name. She has prosecuted and won cases that have set a legal precedent and a new standard for gun accountability in our country. I am incredibly proud of her journey and impact, and I am honored to be her friend!

These stories are meant to inspire, but remember, you are embarking on blazing **your** own trail, which will be unlike any other. Hold tight to an unshakeable belief in yourself, and stay open to possibilities. Defining your *why* will provide a strong foundation for understanding your values and crafting a meaningful professional purpose statement that reflects your authentic self and aspirations.

AFFIRMATION

"I trust my inner voice. She knows."

Define your why
*to serve as your
guiding force*

———

*Align your values
& embrace who you
are becoming*

———

*Set specific goals &
implement systems to
ensure forward progress*

03.
fail
forward

"If you're not making some notable mistakes along the way, you're certainly not taking enough business and career chances."

—SALLIE KRAWCHECK, CEO & FOUNDER

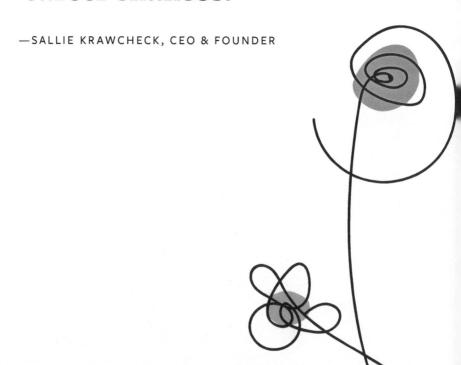

Welcome failure; it signifies that you are taking risks, learning, and growing.

It's time for another mindset shift, and this one is a biggie! Many of us have been taught to be people-pleasers, and to chase the harmony and perfection we see on social media and in popular culture. But to get where you want to go, it will be necessary to take some big swings, fail often, and most importantly *fail forward*.

This chapter will guide you through three key steps to embracing failure as a necessary stepping stone toward growth and success:

1. *Seek Your Discomfort Zone*
2. *Reframe & Honor Your Failures*
3. *Focus on Possibilities, Not Limitations*

Welcoming discomfort and failure as integral parts of the learning process will foster transformative personal and professional growth, and enhance resilience in the face of adversity.

75%

of executive
women report
experiencing
significant fear
of failure[10]

I am going to share one of my most profound mentorship gems. Ready? **The path to confidence lies in <u>action</u>; it requires putting yourself out there, trying new things, taking risks, and, inevitably, experiencing failure.** Too often, when we fail at something, we see *ourselves* as failures. But failure is actually progress in disguise. After all, as the saying goes: "You don't have a chance if you don't **take** a chance." This chapter may require some unlearning. Perhaps you have been taught to play it safe. Perhaps you have internalized that failure is bad. I am here to tell you that failure is necessary.

Why don't we talk about this more? Because we live in a world where perfectionism is portrayed as normal. Social media exhibits a constant highlight reel, showcasing the best days, meals, outfits, flawless teeth, perfect skin, and edited/unrealistic bodies. Social media doesn't show the messiness of life. No one is showing you that this journey is hard, that learning a new skill or job will take time, and that getting it right will require patience and perseverance.

And then there is the "Spotlight Effect". Psychologists Thomas Gilvoich and Kenneth Savitsky coined this term to express the feeling that we are being noticed, watched, and judged much more than we are. In my experience, women are especially prone to this. Fueled by social media, women tend to overestimate how much others notice and care about their failures, which can result in unwarranted feelings of self-consciousness or anxiety.

Trust me, no one is watching you that closely. Consider this example: say you are watching a show on Broadway and everyone is looking at the performers on stage. You're in the audience, munching on popcorn, but when you miss your mouth (oops!), nobody even bats an eye! Why? Because at that moment, no one is watching *you*. Break free by "shifting" the spotlight. Say to yourself, "Oh wait, I'm pointing the spotlight at myself. But it's not always about me." This should empower you to take risks and confidently pursue your goals.

The first step towards this mindset shift is to normalize failure. One of my favorite phrases is, "Sometimes you win, sometimes you learn." Let's start by teaching ourselves how to get comfortable with being uncomfortable, positioning us to take more risks.

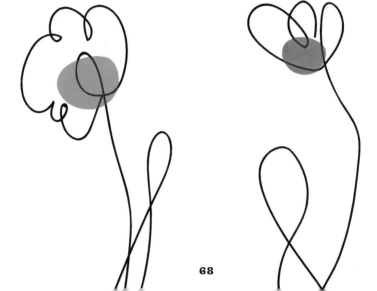

Step 1: Seek Your Discomfort Zone

Taking risks and trying new things is the most important catalyst for personal and professional growth. The objective is to cultivate a mindset that not only embraces discomfort, but also perceives it as a chance for self-discovery, resilience, and broader opportunities. After all, according to *Forbes*, **the #1 action women should take to advance their careers is to move outside their comfort zone.**

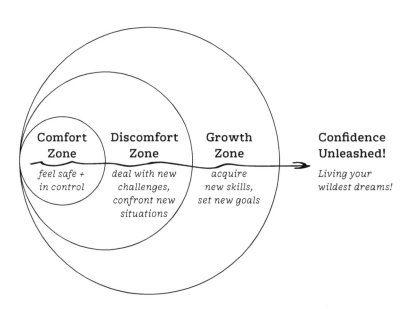

Comfort Zone	Discomfort Zone	Growth Zone	Confidence Unleashed!
feel safe + in control	*deal with new challenges, confront new situations*	*acquire new skills, set new goals*	*Living your wildest dreams!*

78%
of professionals say that moving outside their comfort zone is fundamental to growth and advancement[11]

Storytime! I was 26 years old and had never been on an airplane when I received an offer to join GE's Audit Staff. The Audit Staff was/is considered an elite leadership development program, whereby individuals rotate every four months globally, undertaking diverse business assignments. I had never ventured far from my home in Michigan and felt a huge pit in my stomach. This was an incredible opportunity, but one that was clearly outside of my comfort zone. I had so many questions! What would it be like traveling the world? Would I have the skills necessary to succeed?

I said "Yes" and that leap of faith changed my life. On my first assignment, I was thrown into a GE Plastics factory audit to assess inventory issues. I didn't have expertise in supply chain management. How could I contribute? After expressing concern that perhaps I hadn't been the best pick for this assignment, my manager took me aside and told me to rely on my smarts. He advised me to be curious, ask lots of questions, listen intently, and leverage my critical-thinking skills to figure things out.

I dove in and, following interviews with numerous stakeholders, began to pinpoint a theory regarding the root cause of the problem. I ran tests, used data analysis, and kept going. I delivered my audit presentation and received commendations for the detailed report. I also received constructive feedback on some missing variables in my financial analysis that could be improved.

I persevered, equipped with the confidence that I could figure out the next audit. I continued on the Audit Staff for another five years, traveling to every continent and completing audits ranging from cash controls to quality control. This experience laid the foundation for my career, and I am so grateful that I took the leap of faith into the Discomfort Zone. I now actively seek out new experiences in the Discomfort Zone, knowing it is where the greatest personal growth happens. Keep in mind, that **the path to confidence requires doing hard, scary, and uncomfortable things!**

Challenge

Embrace Your Discomfort Zone

This exercise is designed to help you confront your fears and embrace discomfort. Remember, growth happens outside of your comfort zone! You know the drill. Turn on some Lana Del Rey or find a quiet place!

1. **My Comfort Zone:** In which situations do I feel most comfortable and at ease? Which activities or environments do I typically gravitate towards?

   _____

   _____

   _____

   _____

   _____

2. **My Discomfort Zone:** Which situations or activities make me feel uneasy or uncomfortable? When/where have I avoided taking risks or trying new things?

   _____

   _____

   _____

   _____

   _____

3. **My Fears and Challenges:** What are the specific fears or challenges that prevent me from stepping out of my comfort zone? (Note to self: Be honest and specific about what scares me.)

_____

_____

_____

_____

_____

_____

4. **Set a Discomfort Zone Challenge:** Choose one fear or challenge from your list and commit to facing it head-on. This could be anything from speaking up in class to trying a new hobby, or reaching out to someone new.

_____

_____

_____

_____

_____

_____

5. **Reflect on Your Progress:** After completing your Discomfort Zone Challenge, reflect on the experience. How did it feel to step outside your comfort zone? What did you learn about yourself in the process?

_____

_____

_____

_____

_____

_____

Now, keep going! Set a new Discomfort Zone Challenge every month, and commit to pushing your boundaries and embracing new experiences.

Remember, each step you take outside of your comfort zone brings you closer to personal growth and resilience. Embrace the journey and celebrate your courage along the way!

"Courage doesn't always roar. Sometimes courage is the little voice at the end of the day that says 'I'll try again tomorrow'."

—MARY ANNE RADMACHER, WRITER & ARTIST

Step 2: Reframe & Honor Your Failures

Now that you have learned to embrace your discomfort zone and take more risks, you are sure to experience more failure. Congratulations! (*What*?! You might be thinking!) YES, congratulations. Failure is how you learn. Failure is a necessary stepping stone towards growth and success. So we must view failure as a valuable learning experience rather than a setback, and discover the unexpected opportunities that often arise from rejection. As Dr. Martin Seligman, the pioneer of positive psychology said, "It's not our failures that determine our future success, but **how we explain them to ourselves.**"

Believe me, I've failed more times than I can count. Where to begin? I vividly remember my first presentation to the GE Executive Audit Manager (EAM). I was thrilled with the opportunity! However, just a few minutes into my presentation, the EAM interrupted me, questioning the format. He asked me to redo the pitch and present it at the next meeting. Flush-faced, and on the verge of tears, I left the room. Seeking guidance, I turned to an auditor colleague, who shared the standard GE Audit Staff presentation format and coached me on effective delivery. The lesson was clear: provide the EAM with concise bullet points and a clear call to action.

The experience taught me that, when entering a new environment for the first time, I should do due diligence, leverage my network, and gain insights on the keys to success in that arena. This was a critical lesson that has served me well in my career. Later, I returned to the EAM (take two!) and delivered my presentation. This time, he commended the analysis and later shared my presentation as a best practice. The lesson? Don't be afraid to start over again. You are not starting from scratch, but rather from experience.

Now, when something goes wrong, I debrief on why I failed, what I learned, and how I will incorporate that learning in the future—choosing to adopt a positive and growth-oriented mindset towards failure.

Here are some examples of how I have learned from personal failure and leveraged the learnings for transformative growth:

- In high school, I was cut from the softball team, and so I decided to try track and field. In my senior year, I won the high jump state championship.
- In college, I failed differential calculus, and so I decided to try a leadership development course. It inspired me to earn my masters in the field.
- Upon college graduation, I didn't receive an offer from Estée Lauder, my dream company, so I applied and accepted an offer from GE. This is where I gained the above transformative leadership experiences—and also met my husband!

It's true that in the moment, failure can feel devastating, but remember to honor it as part of your story. Trust that in the future, you will be able to look back and appreciate why it wasn't meant to be.

Growing up, I loved playing basketball. I remember when I first started playing, I laughed when I couldn't even reach the net. I missed more than I made it. I also remember my coach telling me, "When you have a bad shot, don't dwell on it. Learn from it and then let it go. But when you have a good shot, watch the ball go all the way in, and listen as it swishes through the hoop. Then pump your fist in celebration before moving on." It turns out that this advice is relevant in life, too. I make mistakes and fail every single day. I need to quickly extract the learnings and move on. But when success comes, it's important to cherish and celebrate. My favorite way to celebrate is to put on some loud music and do a "victory dance". What about you?

Challenge

Earn Your F.A.I.L. Certificate
(First Attempt In Learning)

We "fail forward" by incorporating our learnings from failure to fuel future growth. Let's activate this lesson with a reflection exercise. Write down your reflections in detail, exploring the lessons learned and the steps you can take to apply them in the future.

Think about a recent failure or setback you experienced. Journal in the space below using these prompts:

What happened?

_____

_____

_____

_____

_____

_____

Why did it happen?

_____

_____

_____

_____

_____

_____

How did it make you feel?

_____

_____

_____

_____

_____

_____

Identify at least one valuable lesson or insight you gained from this experience.

_____

_____

_____

_____

_____

_____

How has this contributed to your growth and development, both personally and professionally?

_____

_____

_____

_____

_____

_____

Congratulations! You have earned a F.A.I.L. Certificate. Complete the certificate below and hang it on your professional vision board! Bonus points for posting it on social media (thus contributing to normalizing failure) with the hashtags #FailForward #ConfidenceUnleashed.

CERTIFICATE
OF FIRST ATTEMPT IN LEARNING

THIS CERTIFICATE IS PROUDLY PRESENTED TO

_____

I FAILED AT

_____

WHAT I LEARNED

_____

HOW I WILL INCORPORATE LEARNING

_____

Fail Forward
Like Reshma Saujani

Remember this number: 580,000 girls. In 2010, Reshma Saujani ran for the United States House of Representatives (NY) and lost her race. *She failed.* Thank goodness! Saujani's experience of losing her congressional race inspired her to found Girls Who Code in 2011. During her campaign, she visited numerous schools and noticed a significant gender disparity in technology classes. Recognizing the importance of addressing this gap, and the transformative potential of coding skills, Saujani decided to take action. She founded Girls Who Code with the mission of closing the gender gap in technology and empowering young women with coding skills. Sparked by her electoral defeat, she was able to leverage her passion for advocacy and education. For over ten years, Saujani served as CEO, impacting the lives of more than 580,000 girls. At the end of 2020, spurred by the pandemic's effect on women's lives, she also became the Founder and CEO of Moms First. Saujani embraces failure. She even posts a weekly #FailureFriday where she spotlights a weekly failure in her life. A recent entry began, "Happy Failure Friday! I'm gonna be honest: I was a hot mess this week." I can relate! I love Saujani's authenticity. Hopefully, her story inspires **you** to embrace failure. As Saujani says, "You never know where failure leads you, so embrace it every time." And remember: 100% of successful people have failed!

Step 3:
Focus on Possibilities, Not Limitations

You may still be feeling uncomfortable about failure. I like to say, "**The best cure to feeling uncomfortable about failing is to fail *more*.**" The pandemic taught us an important lesson—that we must be change-ready and resilient in today's uncertain and complex world. How do I define resilience? It is the ability to bend, but not break when something goes wrong. How do we do that? By adopting a **growth mindset** and believing that our abilities can be developed through dedication, effort, and learning from mistakes.

A wedding photographer is a great example of why we all need to take more shots (literally!) to generate more failures and, consequently, more successes. On average, a wedding photographer captures anywhere from 1,000 to 3,000 photos throughout the Big Day. But they deliver only 50 to 100 shots to the bride and groom. Why? Because they make sure to *over-shoot*; to experiment with lighting, angles, approaches, etc., to produce a handful of 'winning' shots.

"You may encounter many defeats, but you must not be defeated. In fact, it may be necessary to encounter the defeats, so you can know who you are, what you can rise from, how you can still come out of it."

—MAYA ANGELOU, POET & CIVIL RIGHTS ACTIVIST

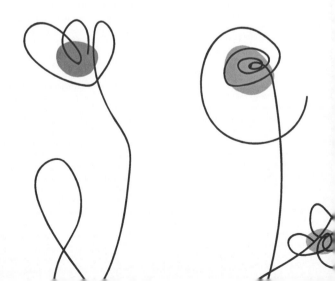

To cultivate a growth mindset, take more shots, and build resilience, we have to shift the focus from limitations to possibilities—and rewrite the narrative. How? One way is to harness *The Power of "Yet"*. Let me explain. "Yet" is a magic word that you can add to the end of any statement to expand your thinking and shift your focus to the possibilities. I recently demonstrated *The Power of "Yet"* to my mentee, Joy. She interviewed for a software engineering internship but wasn't selected because the company was looking for someone familiar with web development frameworks. "I don't have that skill," Joy said. I encouraged her to add the magical word, "yet."

"I don't have that skill... **yet**."

Then we brainstormed ways she could gain experience and master that skill. This summer, Joy will complete a web development course while interning with a government agency to establish an AI Task Force, which complements her desired career path.

Do you see the power?

Here are more examples:

- Unsure about your desired major or career path? "I haven't found my passion... **yet**."
- Feeling stuck in your current role? "I haven't reached my full potential... **yet**."
- Struggling with a difficult project or task? "I haven't mastered this skill... **yet**."
- Facing rejection from a job opportunity? "I haven't found the right fit... **yet**."
- Passed over to lead a team or project? "I'm not in a leadership position... **yet**."

Get it? *The Power of "Yet"* can be transformative; it shifts your focus from failure and limitations to possibilities.

Also, always be sure to tell your story in a positive, uplifting light. Let's try this out.

Challenge

Rewrite Your Narrative

It's time to reflect on a recent failure, use the word "yet" to reframe your thoughts, and then write a new, empowering narrative about the failure. Focus on how you can grow, and what steps you can take to improve in the future.

Here is my example:

My Failure:

> As my college graduation approached, I had my heart set on getting an offer from the Estée Lauder Company. My skills and experience were aligned, and I felt that I had excelled in the interview. However, I did not get an offer. "I don't have a job," I lamented.

Add "Yet":

> "I don't have a job... <u>yet</u>. I will explore other companies that may be a better fit."

Rewrite My Narrative:

> One rejection won't extinguish my fire. Despite the disappointment, I'll channel this interview feedback to propel my growth. I'll seek out other opportunities and secure an offer at a company that resonates more with my values and purpose.

Now, it's your turn!

My Failure:

_____

_____

_____

_____

_____

_____

Add "Yet":

_____

_____

_____

_____

_____

_____

Rewrite Your Narrative:

_____

_____

_____

_____

_____

_____

If you were to ask me what has been most pivotal in my career, I would say this: embracing a lifelong learning mindset and viewing failure as a crucial learning tool. What looks like failure can open the door to the next opportunity—that is, if we fail forward. You can do this, too! Stop looking at successful people as if they've always been successful. Recognize that they are simply individuals who have excelled at navigating through failure. That *is* success. Learning how to deal with failure builds true self-esteem and resilience—two traits that factor directly into success throughout life. So, take your shot, keep showing up again and again, and remember: **You are a marvel, and you have limitless potential.**

AFFIRMATION

"My failures are stepping stones to my success."

*Confront your fears
& embrace discomfort*

———

*Reframe your failures
as learning opportunities*

———

*Build resilience so
you bend, not break*

04.
embrace
imperfection

"The thing that is really hard, and really amazing, is giving up on being perfect and beginning the work of becoming yourself."

—ANNA QUINDLEN, AUTHOR

Break free of perfection and recognize that you are wildly capable.

It's time to tackle one of the most significant internal barriers for young women: perfectionism. This growing and pervasive phenomenon is marked by a perpetual sense of never feeling good enough. The first line of defense in the battle against perfectionism is to gain a clear understanding of its nature. Knowledge is power, after all. Working toward goals, and making mistakes along the way, helps you stretch and grow. Striving for perfection does the opposite.

These following three steps will free you from the pressures of perfectionism:

1. *Challenge Unrealistic Standards*
2. *Cultivate Self-Compassion*
3. *Celebrate Your Achievements*

Once free, you will achieve better well-being and balance, and optimize your personal growth and confidence.

92%
of people
struggle with
some form of
perfectionism[12]

I grew up long before the era of social media, and I can only imagine the immense pressure you must feel due to the constant social comparisons fueled by Instagram, TikTok, and other platforms. According to multiple sources, there is mounting evidence that social media has contributed to the rise of perfectionism with destructive effects on mental health. According to *Harvard Business Review,* Gen Z'ers increasingly hold irrational ideals for themselves, ideals that manifest in unrealistic expectations for academic and professional achievement, appearance, and possessions.[13] In simple terms, Gen Z demands perfection from themselves and *others.*

Let's be clear: Perfectionism is not the same thing as striving to be your best. Perfectionism is not about healthy achievement and growth. Researcher, Brene Brown, makes the smart distinction that healthy striving is **self**-focused—*how can I improve?*—while perfectionism is **other**-focused—*what will they think?*

Perfectionism impedes success. I saw this happen to my mentee, Sophie, a talented graphic designer. I have known Sophie for over five years, and she often sets excessively high standards for herself and her work. She is a creative genius with a beautiful heart but too often doesn't see that. Sophie recently called to talk about a work project. She started the conversation by stating that she was "devastated" that she had failed and disappointed her manager.

"What happened?" I asked. Sophie explained that she had been invited to share a design proposal for a new high-profile client. She worked overtime, meticulously refining every detail of the design, but just couldn't get it "right". She missed both the deadline and the opportunity to be considered. She felt stressed and paralyzed and didn't know what her next steps should be.

Sophie and I then made a plan to move forward. She would submit the design and ask for feedback—knowing it was too late for consideration but that the feedback would help her on future projects. Going forward, she would hold herself to deadlines and time limits. Working through the night was no longer tenable. Finally, she would set realistic standards and focus on progress rather than perfection. Soon after, Sophie received a Creative Achievement Award for a client campaign (nominated by the client!), so I'd say say this approach has made a real difference.

Perfectionism can also contribute to **impostor syndrome**, which can be defined as feelings of inadequacy and self-doubt. (You know, that nagging voice in your head that keeps you from raising your hand in the meeting because someone else likely has a better answer?!) Perfectionists often set excessively high standards for themselves and have an intense fear of failure. When they inevitably fall short of these unrealistic expectations, they may perceive themselves as frauds or believe that their achievements are undeserved, so there is no joy in success and too much self-criticism. This is classic imposter syndrome.

Consider this startling statistic: **7 in 10 teen girls** believe they are **not good enough** or do not measure up in some way.[14] So no, you are not alone if you feel this way.

Women, especially women of color, are the most susceptible to experiencing these feelings due to systemic barriers and biases that undermine their confidence and sense of belonging. Award-winning actress, America Ferrara, provides a good perspective on this: "It's not my fault I feel like I don't belong in this space—everything my whole life has told me that I don't belong in this space. So it's not really imposter syndrome; it's an appropriate reaction to what I've been told by the world. I feel like a stranger in this space because I am a stranger in this space. A lot of us are the first people like us to be in these spaces. So feeling that way is the most appropriate response you can have."

So, let's work on breaking free from perfectionism and imposter syndrome. After all, you have to believe in yourself and your abilities to attract the right opportunities.

75%

of female
executives have
faced imposter
syndrome[15]

Step 1:
Challenge Unrealistic Standards

The first step is to ensure that you are not holding yourself to unrealistic standards. Excessively high standards can fuel a spiral of perfectionism, resulting in unrealistic expectations and hindering progress.

Consider this: Research shows that men often apply for a job when they meet only **60%** of the qualifications, while women apply only if they meet **100%** of them.[16] If there's one takeaway from this book, let it be this: don't hold yourself back! **You are ready enough.** Go ahead and apply for the job.

While in college, I worked as an admissions tour guide. Back then, I aimed for perfection. I studied the 20-page tour script (covering Michigan State University's 5,200 acres) like my life depended on it. On my first day, I stepped to the front of the packed bus, and when the bus started rolling, I picked up my microphone and began speaking confidently. "Welcome to Michigan State University!" As we passed buildings, I easily began reciting information, but then... my mind went blank. I was quiet for a while and then started inserting information in fits and starts, as it came back to me. As the bus came to a stop at the end of the 60-minute tour, I lowered my head in defeat. I was ready to hand in my microphone. I likely just gave the worst tour in campus history. However, as the first parents and students filed off the bus, one parent cheered, "Thanks so much for an excellent tour. Your passion for the university shone through!" She said a few more nice things, and then added, "There are so many facts to learn about this campus!"

"Huh," I thought. I had done a good job on my first tour! I realized that I had set an unrealistic standard for myself, to remember every single fact the first time through. I also realized at that moment that **I didn't have to be perfect to have a positive impact. I was capable enough.**

Do any of these unrealistic standards apply to you?

ACADEMICS: *Feeling the need to load up on advanced classes and excel in every class (even non-major courses!).*

CAREER: *Expecting rapid advancement and success on day one, despite the reality that career progression takes time and involves setbacks; constantly comparing progress to peers or colleagues and feeling inadequate.*

MONEY: *Expecting high salaries or substantial raises early in your career; feeling pressure to achieve financial independence quickly, despite economic challenges and student loan debt.*

WORK-LIFE INTEGRATION: *Striving to achieve a perfect balance between work and personal life from the outset of your career, without recognizing that this balance often evolves and requires adjustments.*

Challenge

Stop Chasing Perfection

It is time to pause and reflect upon the expectations you are placing upon yourself. For this exercise, I recommend playing Pink's song, *Perfect*, on repeat... (♪♪ *Change the voices In your head* | *Make them like you instead* ♪♪)

1. **Reflect on a recent situation where you felt pressure to be perfect.** How did unrealistic standards play a part? How did you react, and what did you learn?

_____

_____

_____

_____

_____

_____

_____

_____

_____

_____

_____

_____

_____

2. **Consider the standards you have set for yourself in your career.** Are they realistic and achievable, or do they tend to be overly demanding? How do these standards influence your approach to work and your overall happiness?

_____

_____

_____

_____

_____

_____

3. **Reflect on the concept of success and how it aligns with your personal values and aspirations.** Are there areas where you can redefine success to prioritize growth, resilience, and well-being over perfection?

_____

_____

_____

_____

_____

_____

Now, repeat after me: _I commit to letting go of the unrealistic standards and pressures that hold me back from embracing imperfection and growth!_ **What we believe, we become.**

Step 2:
Cultivate
Self-Compassion

Recognizing the importance of self-kindness, and prioritizing progress over perfection, is crucial to overcoming perfectionism and impostor syndrome. Perfectionism often leads to self-criticism, perpetuating feelings of inadequacy. To free yourself from this cycle, it is important to cultivate self-compassion. A great place to start? By celebrating incremental progress. My college daughter taught me the importance of 'little treats'. She recently called me to say she had just finished a mid-term exam and rewarded herself with an Insomnia Cookie as a 'little treat'. Yum! My daughter is onto something. Research shows that if you are kind to yourself, and keep an optimistic attitude, you are more likely to reach your goals.

Next, begin to heighten your awareness of self-criticism by tuning into your inner dialogue. Notice when negative thoughts pop up. Learn to rebut with kindness. **The way we talk to ourselves matters.** Also, is it just me, or do most of the negative thoughts and anxiety pop up at night? I have learned to rebut the negative thoughts with kindness, instead thinking, "Okay, Sheri, let's see how we feel about this tomorrow morning." Trust me, anxieties often seem less severe in the light of day.

Challenge

Silence Your Inner Critic

It's time to embrace "good enough" over perfectionism and its accompanying negative thoughts. This exercise will silence the inner voice that holds you back and keeps you small. Start by monitoring your inner dialogue and questioning any negative thoughts about your abilities. Challenge these thoughts by seeking evidence to support or refute them. You'll often discover more evidence of competence than expected. Instead of letting your inner critic control you, aim to assert confidently, "I am truly magnificent and fully prepared!"

Avoid messages that fuel the limiting belief that you are not "good enough" such as:

"What will people think?"

"I'm going to pretend everything is okay."

"I need to excel in every aspect of my academic and personal life."

"If I don't meet society's expectations, I'm a failure."

"I should have everything figured out by now."

"I must always appear confident and put together."

"I should always prioritize others' needs over my own."

"I have to achieve perfection to be worthy of success."

"I shouldn't ask for help; it's a sign of weakness."

Now it's your turn!

- First, identify any similar limiting beliefs you hold.
- Then question these beliefs.
- Finally, reframe them!

Example:

- **Limiting belief:** I need to remember every detail in this 20-page script to be a successful tour guide.
- **Question (Is this belief evidence-based?):** No
- **Reframe belief:** I will strive to do my best, but it's okay to make some mistakes on my first tour. It's most important that my passion for MSU shines through.
- **My affirmation:** I am capable enough.

Limiting belief #1:

_____

_____

Question (Is this belief evidence-based?):

_____

Reframe belief:

_____

My affirmation:

_____

_____

Limiting belief #2:

_____

_____

Question (Is this belief evidence-based?):

_____

Reframe belief:

_____

My affirmation:

_____

_____

Limiting belief #3:

_____

_____

Question (Is this belief evidence-based?):

_____

Reframe belief:

_____

My affirmation:

_____

_____

Now, combine your positive affirmations into an **"Open When"** letter. You will <u>open</u> this letter <u>when</u> you are doubting yourself. End your letter with the statement, **"I am enough, just as I am."**

♥

"OPEN WHEN" LETTER

Step 3:
Celebrate Your Accomplishments

What are you waiting for? It's time to celebrate your accomplishments! Don't wait for external validations like awards or promotions to feel successful. *You* hold the power to recognize and celebrate all your victories, *no matter how big or small.*

Learn to intentionally celebrate and revisit your achievements. Why? Well, our brains have a natural tendency to focus on the negative, which means we often dwell on criticism longer than praise. By celebrating and revisiting your successes, you counteract this negative bias and reinforce positive experiences. This is key to confidence building. So, let's start celebrating!

Challenge

Create A Brag Book

It is time to go through your files! Gather any positive feedback, recommendation letters, gratitude notes, and/or articles, and create a personal Brag Book. Your mom likely did this for you when you were little, and now it's time to take over this practice! Decorate your Brag Book and include the accomplishments that you are most proud of. This can either be a digital or print book. Start now—and commit to growing this book going forward.

Whenever self-doubt creeps in, refer to your Brag Book as a confidence-boosting reminder of past victories.

Things to include in your Brag Book:
>Recommendation/nomination letters
>Positive feedback
>Gratitude notes
>Self-recommendation letter*

*What is a **Self-Recommendation Letter**? Thanks to the "modesty bias," we are more likely to recommend others than ourselves. This phenomenon causes us to underestimate our abilities or qualities, even as we recognize and appreciate them in others. So, get writing... and recommend yourself! (Include at least three accomplishments.)

Now, look in the mirror and read your letter aloud! It can seem silly at first, but hit a power pose in the mirror, and read with confidence!

LETTER OF
SELF-RECOMMENDATION

A peek inside my Brag Book!

Be Your Own PR Agent

One detrimental aspect of imposter syndrome is its tendency to hinder self-promotion. You might find yourself doubting your worthiness of praise. However, it's crucial to advocate for yourself so that others can recognize your value. Why? If managers know your capabilities, then you'll be top-of-mind when opportunities arise. Self-promotion is necessary for career advancement. Unfortunately, women are less inclined to self-promote than men, even for a job. These gender modesty norms are holding us back, and it's time to break free.

These three strategies will enhance your self-promotion:

1. Update your LinkedIn profile with achievements and progress. Embarrassed? Frame these updates as expressions of gratitude to those who have contributed to your success.

2. Nominate yourself for an award. Many awards accept self-nominations, so use initiative to find one that aligns with your accomplishments. For example, I recently encouraged a mentee to apply for a United Way Hometown Hero award, and she won!

3. Volunteer for speaking opportunities or leadership roles at work or in your community. These experiences not only showcase your skills and expertise but also build your confidence in promoting yourself.

Finally, when you give your acceptance speech, channel actress, Niecy Nash-Betts', Emmy award-winning speech: "And you know who I wanna thank? I wanna thank ME. For believing in me, and doing what they said I could not do." It's time to start celebrating our achievements!

"If I waited for perfection... I would never write a word."

—MARGARET ATWOOD, AUTHOR

Get in the habit of celebrating YOU! You are, as *Parks and Recreation's* Leslie Knope said, "a rainbow-infused unicorn!" Embracing imperfection and learning from mistakes will put you on an accelerated path to personal and professional growth.

AFFIRMATION

"I accept the way I am today, versus the way that I'm 'supposed' to be. I am wildly capable of amazing things."

Let go of the unrealistic standards that hold you back from embracing imperfection

———

Show yourself kindness & silence your inner critic

———

Build confidence by celebrating your achievements— big & small

05.
accept
uncertainty

"Uncertainty is the spice that adds flavor to life. Embrace it, and you will find yourself on a journey filled with excitement, growth, and endless possibilities."

—ESTÉE LAUDER

Embrace the unknown to create new possibilities and rewarding experiences.

In the final mindset shift, we will explore the significance of embracing uncertainty, cultivating adaptability, and fostering a curious, open mindset. This mentality is crucial for your career leadership journey. The goal is to stay receptive to opportunities and transform self-exploration into proactive discovery.

This chapter will guide you through three vital steps that will yield an open mindset and the necessary versatility to thrive in today's dynamic, uncertain world.

1. *Value Adaptability*
2. *Cultivate Curiosity*
3. *Pursue Magnificent Possibilities*

Embracing uncertainty will enable you to navigate change, seize new opportunities, and thrive in an ever-evolving professional landscape.

It's undeniable: We live in uncertain times. The pandemic has taught us all this lesson! Yet, despite this, many of us cling to the notion that the path to success is concrete and clear. We humans share a fear of the unknown.

I'd like to introduce a better approach, which I call the **Invisible Staircase**. The Invisible Staircase encourages a **growth mindset by staying open to possibilities.** It underscores the reality that it's impossible to predict the exact steps you'll need to climb or foresee what lies ahead in your career leadership journey.

Of course, not knowing what job you will get upon graduation or feeling unsure about your next career move **is** scary! (According to a survey by the American Psychological Association, nearly half of all adults feel uncertain about their career path.)[18] But embracing the Invisible Staircase means embracing "scary", which creates space for change and growth. The alternative would be letting our fear of the unknown keep us from taking action to move forward.

My Dream Career   **A Fulfilling Career**

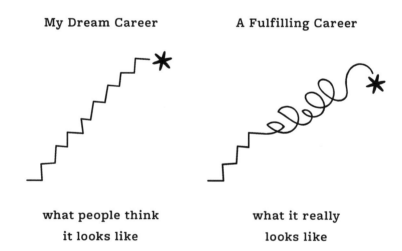

**what people think
it looks like**   **what it really
looks like**

Stepping into unfamiliar territory allows you to develop invaluable qualities essential in any career: resilience, adaptability, and problem-solving skills. Being honest about your lack of certainty—signaling vulnerability—opens up new possibilities. Meditation pioneer, Sharon Salzberg, once said, "It is in the place between the known and the unknown that we find the essential truth." I learned first-hand that uncertainty can cultivate knowing and lead to good things.

Earlier, I shared how I began my career in Corporate America. Leaving my small town behind, I embarked on a journey that took me around the world. Every moment was filled with excitement as I traveled, audited, and embraced new experiences, expanding my horizons in every direction. I didn't mind the long hours, often working late into the night and on weekends. I delved into the realms of manufacturing, finance, and financial services, honing my abilities as a transformative leader. Later, I got married and started a family, overjoyed with my piece of the American dream. Armed with what society considered my ideal career path, I diligently checked off milestones along the way: a good job, global travel, ample training and development opportunities, and rapid promotions with increasing responsibilities.

But my preordained idea of success didn't encompass how to effectively integrate my work and personal life and, with three kids, both started to suffer. So, I decided to take a "career pause" (for one year, I thought) and consider my options. (Note: Women are 43% more likely to take a career break than men, according to LinkedIn.[19] Why don't we talk about this more?!) But taking time out messed with my head. I was unsettled by the uncertainty. Was this "career pause" a step back in my career? I couldn't see up the Invisible Staircase! I labored with the decision-making process and felt tremendous anxiety, not knowing what was to come next in my life. You see, I had lived with a preconceived idea of what my ideal career path would look like, and I was finding it difficult to adapt and change. My "fear of the unknown" had paralyzed me, so that I couldn't even properly brainstorm options.

Soon after, my husband asked me, "If you could do anything and not worry about failing, what would you do?" Wow! This question was revelatory. Ideas started popping into my head about the direction I wanted to take, albeit an uncertain one. As I did so, something happened. I started feeling **elated** about these new possibilities!

Several months later, I committed to the idea of founding a nonprofit women's leadership organization (LiveGirl). I was starting again and, while I was still climbing an Invisible Staircase and didn't know what was next, I did know what was next **in the process.** I would leverage my skills and apply my leadership toolkit to build a business.

In times like these, it's crucial to **adapt and embrace a growth mindset** (which we covered in Chapter 3). Starting my own business would certainly require it!

Looking back, I realize that I stayed on the corporate path longer than I should have because it provided certainty. I was familiar with the job, the promotion cycle, the expectations, etc. But, after accepting uncertainty, pausing, and looking inside myself, I was finally able to embrace who I wanted to become. The uncertainty and the curiosity about **what could be** allowed me to process my experiences, aspirations, and the possibilities ahead. My career pause served as a mental reset, enabling me to explore a whole new world. This is what the saying **"be still and know"** means.

P.S. This book launch will follow LiveGirl's 10th-anniversary celebration. In the past decade, we have served over 18,000 girls, making a substantial impact in shaping future leaders and launching young women into the workforce. And I couldn't be more certain that **this** path was meant for me!

My hope is that you can learn from my experience and accept uncertainty by working through the following three steps. Let's get to it!

71%

of global
executives say that
adaptability is the
most important
leadership quality
in the digital age [17]

Step 1:
Value Adaptability

The goal is to accept and reframe uncertainty as an opportunity for growth rather than fear. By acknowledging that uncertainty is inherent in our lives and careers, we learn to view it as a catalyst for creativity, innovation, and personal development.

Do any of these "I statements" resonate with you? [20]

"I always want to know what the future has in store for me."

"I find it frustrating not knowing what will happen in the future."

"I find it difficult to cope with ambiguous or uncertain situations."

If you answered yes to any of these... read on!

I recently coached my mentee, Brea, about the gift of uncertainty. She graduated with a business degree and landed her "dream job" (her words) on Wall Street. Eighteen months later, when we met for coffee, she shared the news that she realized that she had taken the wrong path. She then said, "Even worse, I don't know what I want to do with my career, and I am falling behind!"

"Wait a minute, Brea," I said. "Can you reframe the uncertainty of your situation by focusing on the possibilities that lie ahead?" Brea paused, and I sensed a shift. "I have learned that I'm not meant for a high-pressure financial analyst position, but I'm excited to explore opportunities in the education or technology sector that would leverage my skills."

Bingo! Let's practice putting this to work.

Challenge

Face Your Fears

Facing your fear of the unknown is crucial to your career journey because it will empower you to embrace uncertainty as an opportunity for growth and exploration. By confronting this fear, you enable yourself to step out of your comfort zone, discover new paths, and develop the resilience needed to navigate through the challenges of the professional world. This mindset allows you to take ownership of your career trajectory, make informed decisions, and pursue opportunities that align with your aspirations and values.

1. **Reflect and describe how you feel about the unknown.**
    <u>Example:</u> Scary! Overwhelming!

    _____

    _____

    _____

2. **Reflect and write down at least three negative beliefs that are related to uncertainty and fear of the unknown.**
    <u>Brea's example:</u> "I am worried that I must have my entire career mapped out before I can take any meaningful steps forward."

    _____

    _____

    _____

3. **Write down at least two actionable steps you can take to adapt and overcome these beliefs.**

   <u>Brea's example</u>: "I accept that I don't have all the answers right now. My career journey will be a process of discovery. As a next step, I will explore job opportunities in the education and technology sector."

   _____

   _____

   _____

   _____

   _____

   _____

   _____

   _____

4. **Take a moment to envision how taking these actionable steps can positively impact your career journey. Write down your thoughts and feelings about the potential outcomes of facing your fear of the unknown.**

   _____

   _____

   _____

   _____

   _____

   _____

   _____

   _____

Be a Versatile Leader

To accept uncertainty, you must be flexible and adaptable in the face of changing circumstances and unknown outcomes. Good news! This new muscle, adaptability, will also help you become a versatile leader. A versatile leader excels at adapting to different situations, harnessing diverse skills, and driving innovation to achieve success in an ever-changing world. Employers value versatile leadership more than ever.

According to the Center for Creative Leadership, **91% of executives believe that versatility, and the ability to lead through complexity and ambiguity, are the key leadership skills for the next decade.**[21] This statistic underscores the importance of versatility in leadership, as leaders need to adapt to rapidly changing environments, navigate uncertainty, and effectively address complex challenges to drive organizational success. In our ever-evolving world, leaders must be ready to pivot when a pandemic strikes or a crisis hits. Organizations thrive when leaders employ versatility to navigate complex challenges, drive innovation, and foster a culture of adaptability."

As Ginni Rometty, former CEO of IBM, said, "Versatility is not just a skill; it's a **mindset** that empowers you to navigate any challenge and seize every opportunity."

Note to self: Become a versatile leader!

Step 2:
Cultivate Curiosity

Recently, I was struck by the term "curious eyes" in Maggie Jackson's book, *Uncertain*. "Curious eyes" means cultivating a gaze filled with inquisitiveness, and a desire to understand the world around you. Research shows that being curious has many benefits, including higher life satisfaction. But how does this relate to your career leadership journey? It involves adopting an open mindset. Trust me, the payoff is worth it. Individuals who exhibit high levels of curiosity are **34% more likely** to achieve high levels of job performance compared to those who demonstrate lower levels of curiosity.[22]

As Sara Blakely, founder of Spanx, said, "Embrace what you don't know, especially in the beginning, because what you don't know can become your greatest asset. It ensures that you will absolutely be doing things differently from everybody else."

It's important to spark curiosity by asking powerful, open-ended questions. For example:

- How can I embrace AI? How is it shaping my company, industry, and world?
- What are some emerging trends or industries that intrigue me, and how can I explore opportunities within them?
- Are there any passion projects that I can pursue to showcase my skills and creativity?

Can you see how being curious in this context might lead to new opportunities? So, let's all develop "curious eyes"!

92%

of professionals view curiosity as a catalyst for job satisfaction, motivation, innovation, and high performance [23]

Challenge

Create A Curiosity Journal

A Curiosity Journal is a great way to cultivate curiosity. I have provided space for three entries below, but I encourage you to expand this practice to a full notebook!

Whenever you encounter something new or intriguing, jot it down in your journal. This could be a thought-provoking article, an interesting conversation, a fascinating lecture topic, or even a random question that pops into your mind.

For each entry, write down what sparked your curiosity and any questions or ideas it inspired. Then, challenge yourself to explore these curiosities further. This could involve researching the topic online, seeking out relevant books or articles, or discussing it with friends or mentors.

Periodically review your Curiosity Journal to track your growth and identify recurring themes or interests.

Curiosity Journal Entry #1
Something new I encountered:

_____

_____

Why it sparked my interest:

_____

_____

Questions/ideas it inspired:

_____

_____

Curiosity Journal Entry #2

Something new I encountered:

_____

_____

Why it sparked my interest:

_____

_____

Questions/ideas it inspired:

_____

_____

Curiosity Journal Entry #3

Something new I encountered:

_____

_____

Why it sparked my interest:

_____

_____

Questions/ideas it inspired:

_____

_____

Step 3:
Pursue Magnificent Possibilities

In your journey, there will be "in-between times" of transition when you feel lost, confused, stuck, or anxious. But be clear—these times of transition are not setting you back. Rather, they allow you to create space and prepare for the next step. This is the time when you pursue magnificent possibilities.

Think about it. Whether you are trying to determine the best approach to solving a problem, navigating a conflict, or identifying the next step in your career, you cannot find the best path forward by assuming that you already know the way. Remember the Invisible Staircase! You have to research, consider options, try new experiences, and then make a decision. What if we reframed this time of uncertainty as a gift; as a time to work toward magnificent possibilities? What if rather than allowing ourselves to be unsettled by uncertainty and rushing to the next step to keep pace, **we slow down to wonder, consider, and explore?**

We all get scared, but **you have a choice** to close in or embrace the uncertainty. The choice to give in or invite trust, and create the opportunity for people to share input and feedback, moving you forward.

I would like to expand on the inspiring journey of my dear friend, Karen McDonald (whom I introduced in Chapter 2). Karen's path led her from a career as a teacher to serving as a judge and, ultimately, becoming the Oakland County Prosecutor in Michigan. Her story exemplifies the transformative power of embracing uncertainty and curiosity, guiding her toward new possibilities. In 2020, after recognizing the importance of avoiding conflicts and perceptions of bias, Karen made the bold decision to step down from her role as a family court judge to run for the office of Oakland County Prosecutor. It was a challenging and uncertain journey, with her job hanging in the balance. However, Karen faced the uncertainty head-on, pouring her heart and soul into the campaign. When I asked Karen about her remarkable journey, she simply said, "I used the uncertainty as fuel. I took a chance on myself and the impact I knew I could make."

Stepping down from the judge's bench to run for prosecutor was a bold move, but Karen didn't look back. She was curious about the impact she could make as a prosecutor (what if?) and aligned her thoughts with who she wanted to become. She started to work toward the magnificent possibility of shaping justice. Her courageous spirit and unwavering determination ultimately led her to victory.

"If one thing is certain, certainty can be comfortable and demand little from us, but clinging to it limits our future, stifles potential, shrinks opportunity, and precludes us from ever realizing just how much we're capable of doing."

—DR. MARGIE WARRELL, AUTHOR OF *BRAVE*

Challenge

Imagine The Possibilities

Consider this quote: "What would you attempt to do if you knew you could not fail?"

Close your eyes and **imagine** yourself fully embracing the uncertainty and working toward magnificent possibilities. Picture yourself exploring new paths, taking risks, and opening yourself up to unforeseen opportunities.

1. How did this visualization make you feel?

_____

_____

_____

_____

_____

_____

2. What actions would you take that you aren't taking now?

_____

_____

_____

_____

_____

_____

3. What conversations would you engage in that you've been avoiding?

_____

_____

_____

_____

_____

_____

4. Where would you step up to the leadership plate more boldly, and in doing so open up the possibility for new opportunities, new relationships, new alliances, and new ideas to take bloom?

_____

_____

_____

_____

_____

_____

_____

_____

_____

_____

Congratulations! You are on your way to experiencing the transformative power of accepting uncertainty, which **will** lead to risk and failure, but also to glorious growth and success. Let go of the fear of the unknown and accept uncertainty as a catalyst for growth.

And just like that... We have concluded the first half of this workbook! Congratulations on cultivating a mindset conducive to your career leadership journey. You've navigated leading with a defined brand and purpose, embracing failure, imperfection, and uncertainty to remain open to opportunities. Above all, these mindset shifts are designed to empower you to recognize your strengths and worth, to trust in your capabilities, and to unleash the incredible potential within you. In the second half, we will focus on building the skills necessary for your continued growth and success. (But first, please enjoy a "little treat" or dance party. Celebrate your mid-point success!)

AFFIRMATION

"I embrace uncertainty as an opportunity for growth and exploration. I trust that the path forward will unfold in unexpected yet magnificent ways."

*Reframe uncertainty
as an opportunity
for growth rather than
a source of fear*

———

*Be open, inquisitive,
& willing to explore
new opportunities*

———

*Slow down to explore
your options & embrace the
magnificent possibilities*

PART II
Build
skill

your

06.
own your career

"Stop waiting. I am blooming whether you water me or not. Whether you offer me light. Whether you stand next to me or not."

—KAREN OWUSU, POET

Focus on what you can control. Show up and invest in yourself.

Here we go! On to the second half of this workbook where we will focus on building skills. Remember the significance of the flower illustrations? In the first half, you prepped the soil and planted the seeds. Now, we will nurture those seeds so they bloom and grow! Remember, it all starts with cultivating the right mindset—one that's ready to take risks, embrace failure, and navigate uncertainty with resilience and confidence. With this mindset, you will now develop the skills necessary to unleash your leadership potential and build an authentic, fulfilling career.

Of course, there are numerous career-readiness skills we must all develop. You may reference the National Association of Colleges and Employers website (naceweb.org) for a comprehensive listing. Here, however, we'll focus on the skills that I've found both critical and daunting for early-career women. For each skill, I'll outline key steps and challenges to help you gain mastery. Oh, the places you'll go once you've built these skills!

Let's start with the importance of "owning your career." What does this mean? Think of it as sitting in the driver's seat. Owning your career means being intentional about who you are and what you want, instituting productive habits, and, most of all, showing up for yourself. By being proactive, **taking charge of your career plan,** and directing your growth and development, you will orchestrate your long-term success and fulfillment. It's up to you to invest in yourself through continuous learning and solid execution to *make that plan happen.*

This chapter will guide you through three ways to take charge of—and **own**—your career so that you have a greater sense of agency **over** your career.

1. *Ask for Feedback*
2. *Adopt Atomic Habits*
3. *Show Up*

These key steps will build the foundational skills of career and self-development, professionalism, and initiative, which will enable you to realize your most ambitious career goals.

70%
increase in likelihood of being promoted when you actively take ownership of your career[24]

Okay, ladies, let's get to the heart of it: You must own your career, because no one else will. Maybe this fact hasn't been clear to you because you've observed peers who seem to land their next jobs effortlessly. The truth is, for some, it's easier due to "who they know." It's unfair, but 91% of college students secure internships through connections.[25] Yes, this reflects systemic bias. Here's another reality check: You might have the connections and university pedigree to facilitate your next career move, or you might not.

So what do you do? First and foremost, focus on **what you can control**. You can't control the weather, the state of the world, the state of your employer, or what other people think and do. But you can control **your actions, your attitude, and your effort.** You can't control the timing of the next leadership opening at your company, but you can make sure that you are prepared for that spot when it does open. (Note to self: Don't obsess over the timing!) When you focus on what you can control, you will find that you generate more wins, and develop a greater sense of agency over your career.

Here is a quick mental exercise to incorporate daily:

- *Morning: Identify 2-3 things you can control today*
- *Evening: Identify one "daily win"*

Here's how I applied this thinking as I prepped to be the host and keynote speaker at a recent LiveGirl Career Discovery event:

- *What I can control:* My preparation, my speech, wearing an awesome outfit that makes me feel confident
- *What I cannot control:* Who attends, their questions, the other speakers' presentations, the weather
- *My daily win:* I killed my speech!

Incorporating this daily discipline to shape your actions, attitude, and effort will generate positive momentum and build resilience. Now we're ready to get into the first action *you can control* as you step up and own your career.

Step 1:
Ask for Feedback

Fact: Once you graduate college and start your career, the learning has just begun! But now, instead of a professor grading your exams and providing feedback, *you* will need to own this step. It's up to you to seek feedback and commit to a plan of continual learning to achieve your goals. Remember, as you grow and change, your world will also change, so there is always more learning to do!

In Chapter 2, I shared how I took a big leap in my career when I applied for—and was accepted into—the GE Corporate Audit Staff. This is an accelerated leadership development program, in which you are given a new assignment every four months. That's a rapid pace, so you quickly learn how to scope an assignment and implement and execute your project plan. At the end of every four months, you present your final work to senior executives and receive a 360-degree feedback performance review. That's a lot of feedback! (The term "360-degree" refers to the idea that feedback is collected from all around you, including superiors, subordinates, peers, customers/clients, etc.) At first, I was taken aback by the considerable amount of feedback...but then I learned the secret. **Feedback is fuel for accelerated growth.** I learned to yearn for feedback. So, when I reached the top of the Audit Staff and was promoted "out" to a business, I was dismayed to see more than a year go by with no performance review or feedback. I have since learned that, while many companies have structured perfor-mance review processes, many do not. What's more, many managers are not skilled at delivering feedback or giving you the information you need to excel in your role. So, you must build your **ask muscle**![26]

If you do not have a manager or environment focused on development, you need to ask for it. After a presentation, project, or major deliverable, be clear that you want honest feedback, and ask for targeted feedback. *Try this*: *"Do you have any feedback for me? What can I do better next time?"* I have learned that if you simply ask a generic question, like "How was that?" you will likely receive an unhelpfully generic answer, "Great!". By asking "What can I do better?" or "What is one thing I can improve?", you will likely end up with a helpful nugget of feedback.

Note: Being intentional about asking for check-ins and feedback is especially important in a remote work environment. Unlike an in-person environment, where you can grab a manager or colleague on the way out of a meeting, you will need to schedule this time if working remotely.

Remember, feedback can sting, but don't take it personally! Soon after starting my first job out of college, a Human Resources manager took me aside and suggested that I think about upgrading my wardrobe to include more professional attire. I felt embarrassed and defensive ("It's the best I can afford!"). But over time, I gained perspective to appreciate the fact that my manager cared enough to give me that feedback. I was the first generation in my family to work in Corporate America, so I lacked the knowledge and resources to appreciate what constituted an "appropriate" wardrobe. There may also be instances where you don't fully agree with the feedback. Again, don't take it personally; listen without judgment, and seek the helpful kernel amidst the feedback provided.

You might also need to ask for clarity on expectations and measures of success. Again, you may have a manager who is crystal clear with this information. In other cases, you will need to flex your "ask muscle". *Try this:* Ask your manager, "What will success look like at the end of this assignment?"

Once you ask for—and receive—both feedback and clear expectations, you can draft your professional development plan. This plan will become your personalized roadmap for skill enhancement, career advancement, and personal growth. It should include a summary of your strengths and development needs, as well as the skills and relationships you need to build to get to the next level. Finally, it should include the key ways you will upskill and learn over the next 12-18 months (e.g., courses, certifications, and experiences). The key is to update your professional development plan annually to allow for your career to evolve in response to the changing world. Just as a business has a strategic plan to guide its course, your professional development plan will encourage you to think ahead and invest in yourself.

Challenge

Build Your "Ask Muscle"

Let's put this to work! First, identify at least two people you may ask for feedback. This can include a manager, peer, subordinate, or others. Then, ask away! Approach the conversation with humility, openness, and a genuine desire to improve.

Try this:

> "I value your perspective and was wondering if you could provide me with some feedback on [specific aspect of your work]. What do you think I could do better or differently?"

Or this:

> "Hi! I admire your expertise in [specific area]. Could you please share any observations or suggestions you have for me to improve my effectiveness in [related aspect of your work]?"

Once you have the answers, it's time to outline your professional development plan. I asked my mentee, Jane, to model this exercise. Let her responses guide and inspire you!

Jane's Example:

> Jane approached her manager and a colleague for feedback. They shared that, while Jane was doing great work independently, she could have an even greater impact by collaborating more with the team to better understand team roles and dynamics. In response, she set the following learning goals and implementation plans.

What I Want to Learn:
- Build deeper connections across the team; better understand different job scopes.
- Expand my technical skills to understand interconnected technologies.
- Expand my business acumen to understand interconnected internal and external business strategy.

Implementation Intentions:
- I will schedule a 30-minute coffee chat with a new team member once a month.
- I will propose 2-3 innovative technical solutions for quarterly projects.
- I will attend one business acumen training from the company website once a month.

Now, it's your turn!

My Feedback & Professional Development Plan

Who I Asked for Feedback (Names):

_____

_____

Summary of Feedback:

_____

_____

_____

_____

My Strengths:

_____

_____

My Development Needs:

_____

_____

What I Want to Learn:

_____

_____

Implementation Intention #1:

"I will _____ at _____ in _____."
       [behavior]   *[time]*   *[location]*

Implementation Intention #2:

"I will _____ at _____ in _____."
       [behavior]   *[time]*   *[location]*

Implementation Intention #3:

"I will _____ at _____ in _____."
       [behavior]   *[time]*   *[location]*

Step 2:
Adopt Atomic Habits

The second step within your control is your discipline to execute. I recently read the book *Atomic Habits* by James Clear, and it changed my life. The book advocates for the power of small changes, aka atomic habits, that can lead to remarkable results over time. The Cliff Notes: Instead of focusing solely on **what** you want to achieve (outcome-based habits), focus on **who you want to become** (identity-based habits). The theory is that our habits shape our identity, and our identity shapes our habits. (I have found this to be true!)

So, how does this magical thinking apply to your career leadership journey? Here's an example. Say it's Thursday night, and you are on the couch binging a Netflix show. You had signed up to attend a networking event, but who can move at this late hour? Stop. Ask yourself, *"What would a person who owns their career do?"* Get up and attend the networking event, that's what! So, put on a cute blazer and go. You can watch your show when you get back.

Let's practice. Think, ***"I am (the person I want to become) and then prove it to yourself.***

Here is my example.

Desired Identity: I am productive, whether working in person or remotely.

Action: I design my environment for success. On the days I work remotely, I separate my work/life by working in a productive, distraction-free space.

Get it? Now it's your turn!

Challenge

Identify *Your* Atomic Habits

Define—and commit to—at least three atomic habits relating to your career leadership journey. Remember, we're talking small, manageable actions that can be easily incorporated into your daily routine. Integrate your new habits into existing routines or rituals to make them easier to remember and stick to. Aim to perform your chosen habits consistently, ideally every day if feasible. Research suggests that repeating an action daily for about **21 days** can help solidify it into a habit. I promise, before you know it, these atomic habits will spark remarkable change. Be sure to celebrate and enjoy a lil' treat after hitting milestone days marked with *!

Desired Identity:

I am someone who owns her career.

Action:

Spend 10 minutes each day on professional development activities (e.g., reading, networking, reflecting, planning).

☐ *Day 1*　☐ *Day 2*　☐ *Day 3*　☐ *Day 4*　☐ *Day 5**　☐ *Day 6*

☐ *Day 7*　☐ *Day 8*　☐ *Day 9*　☐ *Day 10**　☐ *Day 11*　☐ *Day 12*

☐ *Day 13*　☐ *Day 14*　☐ *Day 15**　☐ *Day 16*　☐ *Day 17*　☐ *Day 18*

☐ *Day 19*　☐ *Day 20**　☐ *Day 21*

Desired Identity:

I am committed to continual learning and keeping my skills fresh.

Action:

Spend 15 minutes each day on a learning activity (e.g., podcast, webinar, reading, practicing).

☐ Day 1   ☐ Day 2   ☐ Day 3   ☐ Day 4   ☐ Day 5*   ☐ Day 6

☐ Day 7   ☐ Day 8   ☐ Day 9   ☐ Day 10*   ☐ Day 11   ☐ Day 12

☐ Day 13   ☐ Day 14   ☐ Day 15* ☐ Day 16   ☐ Day 17   ☐ Day 18

☐ Day 19   ☐ Day 20* ☐ Day 21

Desired Identity (Add Your Own):

_____

_____

_____

Action:

_____

_____

☐ Day 1   ☐ Day 2   ☐ Day 3   ☐ Day 4   ☐ Day 5*   ☐ Day 6

☐ Day 7   ☐ Day 8   ☐ Day 9   ☐ Day 10*   ☐ Day 11   ☐ Day 12

☐ Day 13   ☐ Day 14   ☐ Day 15* ☐ Day 16   ☐ Day 17   ☐ Day 18

☐ Day 19   ☐ Day 20* ☐ Day 21

Target Zero Inbox

———

For communications, I utilize the atomic habit of "Zero Inbox". It's true, there are SO MANY WORK EMAILS! (Because every meeting needs a follow-up email... and every follow-up email needs a follow-up email!) How to keep up? "Zero Inbox" refers to the discipline of clearing out your email inbox to zero messages daily. By treating this as a habitual routine, I've found I can maintain better organization, reduce clutter, and enhance productivity. I've also found that it fosters a sense of control and efficiency in managing work-related communications, allowing me to stay focused on important tasks and projects.

Here's how it works for me. I schedule time during my work day (usually 20 minutes late morning and again at the end of the day) to process emails. For quick and easy emails, I respond and delete. For emails that require action, I file in a "Take Action" folder and "Add to Tasks" with a due date. For emails where I need a response to move forward, I file in a "Follow-Up" folder. You bet I will follow up if I don't hear back within 3-4 days! Also key, I "Marie Kondo" my inbox and unsubscribe to any spam emails. Keep your inbox clean! Be sure your personal emails go to a personal address.

Always being slow to respond, or being unresponsive to emails is not a good look! If you are out of the office, or a work project or event makes it impossible to respond in a timely manner, then add an *"Out of Office"* notice. Otherwise, adopting Zero Inbox as an atomic habit will help you build professionalism, trust, and credibility, and help you stay on top of your communications.

Step 3:
Show Up

The final step within your control is how you "show up". This means demonstrating professionalism, competence, integrity, and respect in every aspect of your work. You achieve this by consistently delivering on your commitments and being **present, prepared, and accountable.**

I admire the fact that many of my mentees employ a more casual communication style, and exhibit curiosity by questioning workplace standards. At the same time, it's important to understand the importance of professionalism. Professionalism creates, what I call, **"Career Gravity."** When you "show up" with professionalism, you will attract positive results into your life. In other words, when you demonstrate competence and deliver with integrity and respect, more opportunities will come your way.

So, let's get working on the skills necessary to "show up".

Be present and have *presence*: When in a meeting or conversation, stay off your device and be fully present. (A Center for Professional Excellence study reported that 83% of new hires excessively utilize social media at work. This is not a good look!) When you are fully present, you will have a more impactful *presence.*

Be prepared and accountable: Always proactively prepare. Before a meeting or interview, do the necessary pre-work and anticipate potential questions. I always say, **"Think around corners."** When asking for help, think it through first. Start with "I'm stumped, but here are three ideas on how I might proceed." Take responsibility when things don't go as planned. For instance, I once worked with a young woman advocating for a bill in Congress. She prepared meticulously, but on the morning of the press conference, she overslept and missed it. Despite the setback, she showed resilience by recording a video of her remarks and promptly sending it, along with an apology note, to the Committee Chairman. Her accountability and swift recovery demonstrated her character and professionalism.

Take initiative: Initiative is the ability to take action and make decisions without needing to be told what to do. Don't wait for your big break; create it. Don't wait to be invited to the stage; build your own stage. Don't wait to be selected for an opportunity; create your opportunity. At GE, shortly after being promoted to an Investor Relations role, I found myself thrust into the thick of things during a major investor conference. As I familiarized myself with the team's preparations, I noticed a crucial gap that could potentially derail our efforts. Without hesitation, I took the initiative and approached my boss with a proactive solution. I informed him, "Our timeline is tight, so I've taken the lead on gathering the necessary tabling resources ahead of schedule." This proactive approach not only ensured we were well-prepared for the conference but also showcased my ability to take ownership and drive results. During my first performance check-in, my boss commended me for this initiative. Mission accomplished!

Always follow through: If you promise to do something, do it! If you agree to be somewhere, show up. One of my favorite sayings is, 'undercommit and overdeliver.' I've encountered many young women who, due to their people-pleasing nature, say 'yes' to everything and overcommit. However, this often results in tasks falling through the cracks. As Lean In founder, Sheryl Sandberg, said, "Show up for yourself and be the one who steps in to fill the gaps where things aren't getting done."

Challenge

Ready, Set, Initiate!

These skills take practice! Initiative is a muscle you can build so let's practice with this choose-your-own-adventure exercise.

Select one of the following options:

1. Initiate a conversation with your manager about adding responsibilities to your scope.
2. Initiate a conversation with someone outside of your functional area and ask to learn more about how their role fits into the organization.
3. Initiate a conversation with a colleague who recently completed a successful project and ask to shadow them or learn about their approach.
4. Initiate contact with a more senior person that you admire and request a coffee chat to discuss career advice and insights.
5. Initiate contact with a nonprofit and offer to volunteer your expertise. (Often, volunteering is an excellent way to shine a light on your talents!)

After you complete your action, reflect and journal here, using these prompts:

How did it feel to initiate this action?

_____

_____

_____

What did I learn from this action?

_____

_____

_____

As a next step, what else can I initiate? What would I do if I stopped waiting?

_____

_____

_____

What would I put out in the world if I didn't need permission?

_____

_____

_____

"I am learning every day to allow the space between where I am and where I want to be to inspire me and not terrify me."

—TRACEE ELLIS ROSS, ACTOR & ACTIVIST

Check, done! You are on your way to building the foundational skills of career and self-development, professionalism, and initiative that will enable you to own your career. Do as fashion designer and business-woman, Tory Burch, advises, "Show up, do the work, chase the dream, and never give up." You are sure to be met with opportunities and success as a result!

AFFIRMATION

"My career is a journey, not a destination—and I am in control of it."

3 TAKEAWAYS:

Own your professional development plan that keeps you learning & growing

———

Practice atomic habits that align with who you want to become

———

Show up & demonstrate initiative to generate "Career Gravity"

07.
find your voice

"Speak your mind, even if your voice shakes."

—MAGGIE KUHN, ACTIVIST

Speak up confidently to gain visibility and credibility.

Ok, ladies. You have put in the work and added some important mindset shifts and skills to your toolkit. Now, it's time to shine by unleashing the power of your voice. Finding your voice encompasses more than just speaking up confidently; it involves mastering the art of communication, which includes public speaking and executive presence. Never heard of **executive presence**? I define it as speaking up with poise, confidence, and credibility, and possessing the ability to command attention and influence others. It's no wonder this is a necessary skill for career advancement!

I've observed so many brilliant young women opt out of opportunities involving public speaking, leading them to miss out on valuable experiences and advancement. It's not enough to have value-added thoughts; you need to articulate them confidently in various professional settings—from team meetings to public presentations. Finding your voice entails honing your ability to communicate your ideas persuasively, engage audiences with clarity and conviction, and project a commanding presence that garners respect and attention.

This chapter will guide you through three steps to finding your voice—and using it.

1. *Trust Your Opinion*
2. *Prepare to Shine*
3. *Advocate for Yourself*

When you unleash the power of your voice with clear and effective communication, you will amplify your influence, create future opportunities, and position yourself as a capable leader within your organization.

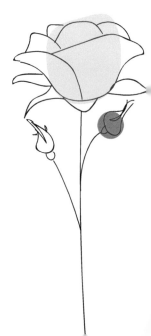

96%
of employers cite communication as the most important career competency [27]

When I was a little girl, I loved being center stage, whether it was performing at Miss Carol's School of Dance or singing Oliva Newton-John's songs at family parties. I loved it all—the costumes, the performances, and commanding the room. But when I started middle school, I was asked to give a presentation and, instead of jumping at the opportunity, I felt scared and anxious. What had happened to all that confidence?

From the outside, it's almost as if young women suddenly learn to be afraid of public speaking. In reality, it's societal conditioning, gender stereotypes, and cultural expectations kicking in. From a young age, girls receive subtle messages that discourage assertiveness and self-expression, while boys are encouraged to speak up and take charge. Consider these common gender messages we absorb as we grow up:

BOYS/MEN	GIRLS/WOMEN
• *Strong*	• *Caring and nurturing*
• *Not okay to cry or express emotions*	• *Emotional*
• *Into building, cars and trucks, bugs, mud, etc.*	• *Interested in fine motor work, like drawing*
• *Interested in large motor play*	• *Providing unpaid or low-paid labor—like childcare, cleaning, cooking*
• *Only okay to be nurturing in some settings—i.e., Being a dad is valued, but not a nurse*	• *Expected to be an advocate and feminist*
• *Expected to lead*	• *Responsible for taking care of everyone*

Source: Julie Nicholson, PhD, and Nathanael Flynn, MA. *Supporting Gender Diversity in Early Childhood*. Redleaf Press, 2021.

These societal norms often create barriers to confidence and assertiveness in public speaking for women and girls, reinforcing a cycle of fear or reluctance to speak out. Have you noticed that men are called upon—and speak—more often than women in the classroom and boardroom? Research shows that in mixed-gender group discussions, men tend to dominate the conversation, speaking significantly more frequently and for longer durations than women. Specifically, **women, when outnumbered, speak as much as 75 percent less than men.**[28] Ugh!

As a teenager, I was no different from most girls, but I was determined to overcome my fear. And so I pushed myself to run for Student Council President, challenging myself to speak at the podium more frequently. All that practice paid off. During my time at GE as an Investor Relations Analyst, I regularly delivered presentations to large groups of people. It was in this demanding environment that I came to realize the importance of public speaking as a skill—one that required consistent practice to master.

Speaking up and asserting yourself is crucial to being seen, heard, and valued. It's important to note that finding your voice doesn't mean dominating discussions. Inclusive leaders listen attentively, foster dialogue, and ensure space for all perspectives, while also sharing their own.

Let's dive into the first step, and start reclaiming your voice.

Step 1:
Trust Your Opinion

Let me ask you: Have you ever had an idea but kept it to yourself? (Be honest!) The key to speaking up is trusting your own opinion and **believing that you have a genuine contribution to make.** Your voice matters—and your silence is an important missing voice. In Chapter 1, we identified your Unique Selling Point and recognized the value you bring to the table. Hold onto this—and trust that your perspective adds value and may inspire others.

Also, learn to trust that your opinion deserves to be heard, no matter what others may think. Consider this fact: **1 in 2 girls doesn't speak her mind because she wants to be liked.**[29] According to the 2019 "Speak Up" survey by researchers Megan Reitz and John Higgins, fear of upsetting others—and fear of being perceived negatively—are the most common reasons people stay silent.

Does this apply to you? Look at the list below, and then ask yourself if you worry about being labeled one of these adjectives.

- Aggressive
- Bossy
- Bitchy
- Smug
- Rude

Now ask yourself this: Would you ever label a man who speaks up in a meeting as overly aggressive? No, right?! So, push back on these double standards. The bottom line is this: Holding yourself back hurts one person only... you! It's time to break free from these fears and speak your mind.

How you think about yourself drives how you speak. So, let's reach back to Chapter 6, where we introduced the concept of identity-based "atomic habits". We all have habits around the way we speak up. The reality is, as a young career woman, your habit may be to defer to others with more experience—or to suppress your ideas because you don't want to be considered "hysterical" or "overbearing". Stop! Let's replace this old habit with a new identity-based habit:

Desired Identity: I am the sort of person who trusts her opinion and speaks up with value-added ideas.

Action: I will raise my hand and speak up in meetings.

Now, let's put this into practice with a Challenge.

Challenge

Learn to Value Your Voice

Take a moment to identify a topic that's important to you, and then take action. Examples include asking for feedback or suggesting an idea at work.

What I'd like to speak up about:

_____

_____

What is holding me back?

Identify what is causing you to distrust the value of your opinion: voices of doubt, other people in positions of power, or the context in which you will have to speak up.

_____

_____

- **Voices of doubt (self-doubt):**

_____

- **Voices of doubt (other people):**

_____

- **Context (environment):**

_____

Why is it important that I speak up?

_____

_____

What are the risks?

What is the worst thing that could happen?

_____

_____

How can I overcome what is holding me back?

If you are experiencing self-doubt, challenge your negative self-talk. If other people in power are causing doubt, first remind yourself they were in your position once, and then seek out mentors or allies for support. If the environment is to blame, work on creating a safer space by building relationships and finding like-minded colleagues.

_____

_____

Now, define a new "atomic habit" to value your voice and take action.

Desired Identity:

_____

_____

Action:

_____

_____

Be Seen Behind the Screen

Virtual meetings have become a staple of modern work life, whether you're working in-person or remotely. While I value the interactive features like chat, Q&A sessions, breakout rooms, icons, and virtual whiteboards, there are drawbacks. I frequently observe participants becoming distracted or multitasking during Zoom calls. Plus, it's more challenging to interpret a coworker's body language when communicating through a screen.

To boost your presence during virtual meetings, try these suggestions:

1. **Turn your camera on!** According to research by psychologist, Albert Mehrabian, **55% of your message is communicated visually through your body language.** And, women's leadership platform *Her New Standard* advises, "Speaking over the phone or disabling your camera during group meetings may be more convenient, but to enhance your leadership presence and maximize your ability to communicate effectively, make sure your camera is on for meetings whenever possible."

2. **Be Zoom interactive.** Because active listening/body language is harder to translate, use a "🤍" emoji to show your support for an idea, or write "love that idea!" in the chat.

3. **Gently interrupt when necessary.** I have been on many Zooms when someone hogs the limelight. If the "raise your hand" feature doesn't work, I suggest gently interrupting. Try saying something like, "George, I'd like to jump in."

4. **Meet IRL if possible.** At the end of the day, nothing compares to IRL team building. If possible, schedule an in-person check-in or a chat over coffee.

Step 2:
Prepare to Shine

Both speaking up and public speaking **are** scary for many of us. So let's take a closer look at what's behind the fear. What prompts you to think, 'I have something to say,' only to be followed by, 'but what will happen if I say it?'

Perhaps your mind magnifies the awful, scary, worst things that could happen...your audience laughs...ignores...or disagrees with you.

SCARY THOUGHTS

Trust me, I have experienced every one of these scary thoughts, but I have also learned that they are overinflated in my head. Sure, I have had some awkward receptions, but never an outcome that I couldn't handle.

If you put in the work and plan what to say, your confidence will soar. Speaking up is like any other skill—a muscle you have to train. Think like a Broadway actor. Would you perform for an audience before rehearsing? No way! So, rehearse what you will say. The more time you spend preparing, the greater your executive presence will be. In short, you will *shine.*

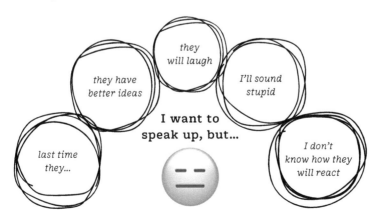

INTRODUCING THE 5 Ws FRAMEWORK

This handy technique will help you proactively prepare and boost your executive presence and confidence. Executive presence is the combination of poise, confidence, presentation skills, and the ability to inspire and influence others. Consider this fact: A *Harvard Business Review* study found that 45% of women said being perceived as having executive presence was more important to being promoted than having specific qualifications.[30] So, prepare to shine by asking yourself the following questions:

WHY: *What outcome am I seeking?*
WHO: *Which stakeholders should be involved? Who has the power to support and act on what I say?*
WHERE: *Which environment (e.g., private vs. group, in-person vs. call, etc.) will be most effective?*
WHEN: *What is the best timing (consider both the urgency and when the other person will be most inclined to listen)?*
WHAT: *What exactly will I say?*

Here's an example of the *5 Ws Framework* in action: In the early 2000s, I was working as a GE Executive Audit Manager when I received the happy news of my first pregnancy. But my celebration pivoted to anxiety at the thought of informing my manager, considering the company's less-than-stellar track record in supporting working mothers. Back then, family discussions were rare among senior female executives. As my pregnancy became visible, I found myself fielding numerous unwelcome comments and questions. One incident, involving a colleague joking openly about my pregnancy, was particularly upsetting. At that moment, I resolved to speak up.

WHY: *Pregnant women deserve respect*

WHO: *My Corporate Audit Staff Director and Human Resources Manager*

WHERE: *A private meeting with the two managers*

WHEN: *First available*

WHAT: *"I'm pregnant with my first child and excited about this new chapter. However, I'm concerned that our workplace culture lacks support for expecting mothers. For instance, I've received uncomfortable comments and questions about my pregnancy. I believe it's important to foster a more inclusive environment. Can we discuss ways to improve our policies and culture to support pregnant women like myself?"*

Fortunately, my managers were receptive—they implemented a plan for small-group conversations and sensitivity training. Success!

Once you speak up more, you'll enhance your visibility, which is a crucial factor in advancing your career. **Career visibility** refers to the extent to which your skills, contributions, and accomplishments are recognized and known within your organization. It encompasses your reputation, influence, and perceived value. I love this advice from LiveGirl Advisor, Shaz Kahng, "My advice on increasing visibility in meetings (whether virtual or in person) is to make an insightful point early in the discussion and do it memorably. Think of something strategically significant and come up with a sound bite that people will remember and repeat. This sets the stage for the rest of the conversation and identifies you as a leader."

I promise, over time you will gain more confidence in speaking up. You may never banish the "butterflies" in your stomach—I still haven't!—but, remember, anxiety occurs because you **care** so much about doing a good job.

Now, it's your turn!

Challenge

Craft a "Speak Up!" Plan

Practice makes perfect. For this choose-your-own-adventure, you will commit to—and prepare for—a speaking engagement. This could be an oral presentation at work, in your community, at a conference, or a written thought piece on LinkedIn. If you are looking to engage more with your community, why not double the impact and share your expertise with a local nonprofit? Trust me, nonprofits are always looking for professionals to share their expertise. Are you a finance analyst? Volunteer to speak at a local boys & girls club about financial literacy. Are you a graphic designer? Offer to lead a free resume-writing workshop at a local nonprofit.

Prepare presentation aids (e.g., slides, index cards, etc.) that will enhance the clarity of your presentation. Before the big day, record your presentation and view the playback, taking notes on your executive presence (especially tone, speed, and enthusiasm), and use of public speaking pitfalls, such as:

- **Overuse of "filler words" ("uh", "um," "you know," and "like")**
- **Phrases like "kind of" and "sort of" that weaken your statements**
- **Disclaimers: "I'm not sure if this is right, but…"**

My Speak Up! Plan

Where I will speak:

- At Work
- In My Community
- Industry Conference/Panel
- Linkedin/Blog Post

When:

_____

_____

Topic:

_____

_____

Presentation aids:

_____

_____

Notes from my recording:

_____

_____

Ways I can improve (note tone, speed, pitfalls, clarity, and enthusiasm):

_____

_____

Now you're ready to shine!

Appreciate Cultural Differences

Cultural differences can impact communication. Taking up space may be especially uncomfortable for some because of their faith or culture. If you fall into this camp, your *Speak Up! Plan* may require extra steps. One of my mentees, Sabrina, really struggled with public speaking because her Muslim faith and family culture prevented her from speaking up. "In my family, women are not supposed to be loud," Sabrina told me. So, together, we crafted a *Speak Up! Plan* with specific goals. First, she took a journal into class and wrote down what she wanted to say. Next, she set a goal of speaking up in a meeting at least once a week. She progressed the goal to daily until, one day, she called me to say she had just given a presentation to her boss. Mission accomplished!

We are all responsible for recognizing and nurturing diverse communication styles. Whether it's a cultural difference, or simply an introverted person who doesn't freely speak up, all of us are responsible for embodying Cultural Intelligence (CQ). This involves understanding behaviors that are culturally determined and sensing how the personalities you interact with both differ from—and reflect—those in your home culture. This is imperative in a global environment. For example, when I was based at GE Capital Information Services in Delhi, India, I had to learn new cultural social cues to fully comprehend the business operations. This meant understanding the significance and context behind local leaders expressing themselves through head nods or "bobbles." Developing Cultural Intelligence is essential to effectively finding and using your voice.

Step 3:
Advocate for Yourself

Finding your voice to champion yourself in the workplace is crucial for several reasons. Firstly, it allows you to assert your ideas, opinions, and contributions, leading to greater visibility and recognition. Secondly, advocating for yourself fosters self-confidence, and empowers you to pursue opportunities for advancement and growth. It is essential for your personal and professional development.

Early in my career, I was fairly quiet (I bet many of you who know me now are shaking your heads in disbelief!). I assumed that because everyone was more experienced, they had better ideas than me, so I stayed mostly silent. However, once I recognized my Unique Selling Point (USP), I began to contribute more. The more I contributed, the more confidence and visibility I gained, which encouraged me to contribute even more—it became a positive cycle.

But even with that success, I held onto the misconception that if I put my head down and delivered, success would naturally follow. Except that wasn't the case. I learned the hard way that your manager won't necessarily advocate for you when it comes to promotions, raises, or other opportunities. It wasn't until years later, when comparing salary notes with a peer, that I realized how far behind I'd fallen. It was then that I acknowledged the truth: you don't get what you don't ask for. So, I decided to step up, take charge, and advocate for myself.

One other thing this experience taught me? The importance of 'managing up'—by which I mean not waiting for your boss to ask for information, or assuming that they are aware of your latest accomplishments. One effective strategy is to proactively provide your manager with a recent list of wins ahead of any HR review. This ensures they're well-informed and positioned to speak to your impact.

Sometimes, advocating for yourself means having **hard conversations.** Often, I see women hesitating to advocate for themselves because they worry it might not seem "nice." However, as author and wellness educator, Alex Elle, said, "Being kind doesn't mean I won't advocate for myself." Your self-care and kindness towards others should not come at the expense of your own well-being and boundaries.

Necessary hard conversations include:

- Negotiating a raise or promotion
- Addressing conflicts or issues with colleagues or supervisors
- Discussing work-life balance or accommodation needs
- Declining additional responsibilities or tasks that may overload you
- Communicating boundaries or concerns

You will shine extra bright as a leader by finding your voice and communicating effectively through these conversations. So, let's practice!

Challenge

Navigate Tough Talks

In this challenge, you will practice the art of creating space and moving the conversation forward. These are necessary skills to advocate for yourself when the talk gets tough.

First, choose one of these scenarios:

Scenario #1: You're embroiled in a conflict with a coworker and it is affecting your work. You need to plan a conversation to address the issue and find a resolution.

Scenario #2: You want to attend a conference, take a course, or get involved in a new project to enhance your skills. You need to convince your manager to support your development.

Scenario #3: You're ready for a promotion. You've checked off all of the boxes for the next senior position, but have been passed over several times.

Scenario #4: You experience, or witness, microaggressions in the workplace.

Now, use the *5 Ws Framework* (Step 2) to think through your conversation and plan what you will say, using the following script as guidance. I strongly recommend the use of "I" statements, which will help you communicate your concerns, feelings, and needs without blaming others or sounding threatening. E.g., "I feel underutilized when..."

Sample Script Intro:

"Thank you for meeting me today. I want to discuss
_____."

I feel [emotion]

_____

When [situation or behavior]

_____

Because [reason or impact]

_____

I would like [desired outcome or action]

_____

Be specific with your request or concern, and provide specific examples to support your points. Listen generously.

Sample Script Closing:

"Thank you for your time. I really appreciate you listening, and look forward to a follow-up discussion."

This practice will help you hone the right words for your next hard conversation. By using "I" statements, you can effectively advocate for your career needs while maintaining a positive and professional tone. Organizational psychologist, Adam Grant, emphasizes that hard conversations are rarely as unpleasant as we expect. His research shows that we often fixate on what could go wrong while overlooking what might go right. Go ahead, you've got this!

Use Intentional Language

Truth time! I laughed recently when I saw a TikTok, showing a woman at her laptop with the caption, "Choosing which sentence in an email gets an exclamation mark so I come across as friendly but professional."

As the cartoonist, Judy Horacek, put it: "What's the difference between being assertive and being aggressive? Your gender." Unfair! Gender stereotypes still hold that men should be dominant and assertive, while women should be kind and caring—and when women violate these stereotypes, they often get punished (aka judged as less hirable).

What to do? Be aware of your audience and be intentional with your language.

Use power language to sound more authoritative:

- **Don't apologize:** "I'm sorry, but I disagree." Replace with,

"I disagree because..."

- **Don't undermine your expertise:** "I feel like..." Replace with, "My research (or experience) has shown me that..."
- **Show confidence in your decisions:** Instead of, "I think we should...," say, "We should..."

Use tentative language to express collaborative interests when advocating:

- **Asking for a raise or promotion:** "I'm hopeful you'll see my skill at negotiating as something important that I bring to the job."
- **Seeking feedback:** "I'd appreciate your thoughts on this."
- **Building consensus:** "I think we might want to consider this approach."

Balancing your language allows you to assert your ideas while maintaining a collaborative and approachable demeanor.

"Silence is the missing voice in conversation."

—MEGAN REITZ AND JOHN HIGGINS,
AUTHORS OF *SPEAK UP*

"EXCUSE ME, I'M SPEAKING."

Do you remember candidate, Kamala Harris's, polite-but-firm response to being continuously interrupted during the 2020 vice presidential debate? I sure do! According to a study by UC Santa Barbara and UCLA, **men are three times more likely to interrupt a woman** than another man during group discussions. So, be ready to assert yourself and hold your ground. Personally, I love VP Harris' response ("Excuse me, I'm speaking.") or you can try, "Hold on a moment, I'd like to complete my idea, and then we can discuss further."

When you find your voice and communicate confidently, your words and ideas will be more persuasive, giving you increased visibility and credibility. After all, you deserve to shine—so step into your power and let your brilliance light up the room.

AFFIRMATION

"I will use my voice unapologetically because what I say matters."

3 TAKEAWAYS:

*Know that
your voice matters*

———

*Put the work in to
speak up & increase
your career visibility*

———

*Have the hard
conversations &
champion yourself*

08.
invest in relationship currency

**"Surround yourself
only with people
who are going to
take you higher."**

—OPRAH WINFREY

Nurture relationships to accelerate your career goals.

It takes a village, not just to raise a child, but to build a career. To succeed, you need to surround yourself with a vibrant support network of coaches, mentors, sponsors, and allies. The goal is to establish a support system that not only propels your career but also ensures that you are championed and supported, even when you're not in the room.

You've likely heard and read a lot about networking, but this chapter focuses on the skill of building strategic relationships—aka **relationship currency.** The term was popularized by business executive and bestselling author, Carla Harris. It's best defined as this: the value and trust built by investing in meaningful professional relationships, which can be leveraged to achieve career advancement and access key opportunities.

This chapter will teach you three ways to build relationship currency.

1. *Invest with Intention*
2. *Build a Personal Board of Directors*
3. *NetWORK & Nurture*

A strong support system that accelerates your professional growth opens up opportunities for career advancement, and serves as the foundation for long-term success and fulfillment.

80%

of women use networking to drive career success[31]

Over the years, I have learned that the type of support we all need varies, even from one day to the next. Early on in my career, I needed mentors to guide my choices on simple things, such as appropriate work attire. Later, I realized that my career progression wouldn't happen on its own and that I needed to secure sponsors who recognized what I brought to the table. I wouldn't have made my biggest career leap at GE—from the entry-level leadership development program to its elite Audit Staff—without a sponsor. My senior manager recommended that I apply, and then called the hiring manager and urged him to hire me. Returning from my first maternity leave, I needed allies who could help ease my transition back and advocate for my needs. Finally, when I decided to leave Corporate America and establish a nonprofit, I needed as many advisors as possible ("all hands on deck!") to successfully make the transition. So I leaned on the network that I had cultivated throughout my corporate career—for advising, strategic planning, funding, and partnering. I certainly could not have done it on my own.

One advisor who played a crucial role during this transition was Amy Rochlin, a seasoned professional with a long and accomplished career in the nonprofit sector. Initially, I reached out to Amy for strategic advice. Later, I came to realize that it was her uplifting, positive spirit—as well as her career smarts—that made her such a powerful confidante. Taking a significant risk was daunting, and Amy's encouragement fueled me forward. I have saved voicemails she left me a decade ago, and I still listen to them when I need a confidence boost!

Over the years I've leaned on support from different sources at different times for different challenges. I have learned that my success depends on seeking advice and being intentional about leveraging my network. My relationships have served as a strong foundation, able to withstand challenges and propel me toward greater heights.

So, let's jump into the first step and start building your support system.

Step 1:
Invest with Intention

To be clear: This is not a contest about who has the most followers on Instagram or LinkedIn. "The key to a good network is depth, not breadth, and you make deep networks with **intentionality**," says Emily Dickens, Chief of Staff and Head of Government Affairs at the Society for Human Resources Management. You must develop **purpose-driven connections** built on trust and shared goals.

The first step is understanding **who** should be in your support network. So, let's start by breaking down the three types of relationships you need in your network: coaches, mentors, and sponsors. Simply put, **a coach talks *to* you, a mentor talks *with* you, and a sponsor talks *about* you.** It's important to understand these different roles and identify who is playing which role for you. For example, you don't want to approach a sponsor (someone who can make a career opportunity happen for you) and discuss work struggles. Rather, you want to highlight the skills you bring to the table so that when the next opportunity arises, your sponsor can advocate for you.

Let's dive deeper into these definitions.

Coach: A career or confidence coach asks powerful questions to help you find your own answers and overcome limiting beliefs. Unlike mentorship, coaching is often a paid, one-sided relationship focused on specific goals over a set period. Some nonprofits (like LiveGirl) provide free-of-charge coaching.

Mentor: A mentor is an experienced professional who offers guidance, advice, and feedback based on their lived experience to help you overcome challenges and navigate your career journey.

Sponsor: A sponsor is a senior stakeholder who uses their connections and reputation to directly endorse and champion you, taking personal risks to provide exposure to better career opportunities.
One more, Ally: An ally is a supportive colleague who will advocate for your professional growth, provide guidance, and/or help navigate workplace challenges.

Now, here's the thing. You need **all** four types of professional relationships in your support network **and** it will take time to develop these relationships. Some you'll meet through serendipity, while others you'll actively seek out through networking. (See Step 3!) But here's the beauty: When you build these strategic relationships, you will activate the power of relationship currency and motivate people to act on your behalf.

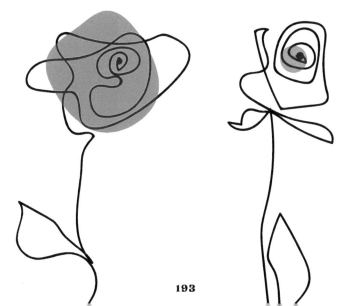

Behold the Power
of Relationships

Connections are crucial for engagement and well-being. Relationships can significantly impact your health, productivity, and resilience. Though developing and maintaining them requires effort, the benefits make it worthwhile. A study in *Nature Human Behaviour* shows that relationships significantly strengthen your resilience in the following ways:

A well-developed network can:

- Help us make sense of people or politics in a given situation
- Help us find the confidence to push back and self-advocate
- Help us recover from mistakes
- Help us see a path forward
- Provide empathetic support so we can release negative emotions

- Help us laugh at ourselves and the situation
- Remind us of the purpose or meaning of our work
- Broaden us as individuals so that we maintain perspective when setbacks happen

To drive this point home, reflect and think about the last time you faced a significant challenge or setback. How did your relationships help you navigate this difficult time? What valuable lessons about relationship management and resilience did you learn?

Challenge

Leverage the Relationship Currency Matrix

It's time for you to identify **who** you need in your support network. For this exercise, we will utilize the Relationship Currency Matrix. This concept was developed by Christine Laperriere, an executive leadership coach and author of *Too Busy to Be Happy: Using Emotional Real Estate to Grow Your Work-Life Wisdom* (and fellow Michigan State alumna! Go Green!). It's a useful tool for evaluating and categorizing professional relationships based on two factors: the level of **trust** and the level of **value exchange**.

RELATIONSHIP CURRENCY MATRIX

HIGH

High Trust/ Low Value: *Trusted relationships that may need more focus on value exchange.*

High Trust/ High Value: *Key supporters who are crucial to your career development.*

TRUST

Low Trust/ Low Value: *Relationships that might not be worth significant investment.*

Low Trust/ High Value: *Valuable connections where you need to build more trust.*

LOW

LOW

VALUE

For each professional relationship, ask the following questions:

1. **Level of Trust**

   Who do I feel comfortable discussing my career aspirations and challenges with? Who has given me honest and constructive feedback? Who has shown genuine interest in my personal and professional growth?

2. **Level of Value Exchange**

   Who has provided me with valuable contacts, opportunities, or resources? Who has shared their knowledge and expertise with me?

Now, fill in the matrix. Pay attention and focus on the relationships in the High Trust/High Value sections.

RELATIONSHIP CURRENCY MATRIX

Step 2:
Build a Personal
Board of Directors

Now that you have identified the key players in your support network (coaches, mentors, sponsors, and allies), the next step is to activate this collective power. To do this, you will develop a 'Personal Board of Directors', drawing inspiration from the corporate world, where CEOs rely on a diverse and skilled board for guidance.

Part of this exercise involves recognizing your weak spots and vulnerabilities—and openly sharing them. You must be able to approach someone and say, "I need help with X." Many of us are conditioned to avoid discussing our weaknesses or failures, but sharing these concerns with someone you respect can open **pathways to progress.** As Keith Ferrazzi writes in *Who's Got Your Back,* "One thing I've learned is that when we allow ourselves to be vulnerable—when we expose our true inner selves to colleagues, with all our strengths and weaknesses, all our accomplishments, skills, and failings—we create an electric connection that leads to trust and intimacy as nothing else does."

The more you open up about your needs, the more people will offer to help. Trust me, people really *do* want to help.

After I decided to launch LiveGirl, the very first thing I did was take inventory of my strengths and weaknesses, and identify skill gaps. Then I created a list of possible stakeholders that I could recruit to help and serve on my Personal Board of Directors. Finally, I began to cultivate relationships, strategically and intentionally. I made a point to attend the same events as my potential stakeholders, and I created opportunities to meet them in person. I wasn't afraid to ask anyone for help. While I had strong business and leadership skills, I knew I needed to enlist experts in youth leadership and nonprofit management. As we looked to grow and expand, I added several Corporate executives who could leverage their networks for LiveGirl's benefit.

Then I established a LiveGirl Advisory Council. Here, I was looking to leverage specific, strategic skill sets to contribute expansive thought leadership. For example, one advisor I brought aboard was Simone E. Morris, an inclusive leadership and career expert. Today, Simone and I have a mutually beneficial relationship and support each other's endeavors. She provides me with important advice, and last year I served as a judge on her inaugural Inclusive Leadership Impact Awards. Together, we co-facilitated a Women's Day corporate roundtable. I am deeply grateful to all of the talented and brilliant leaders who serve on LiveGirl's Board of Directors and Advisory Council.

Note: Be sure to include "fresh eyes" on your Personal Board of Directors. I see many young women relying exclusively on family and friends for advice, but often, your innermost circle is too close to offer unbiased advice. To avoid surrounding yourself with "yes people", it's important to cast a wider net. "Fresh eyes" can give you a jolt of confidence, expanding your view of possibilities.

"One of the best career moves I ever made was building a personal board of directors. Surrounding myself with mentors, sponsors, and peers who provided guidance, support, and honest feedback has been invaluable for my growth and success."

—INDRA NOOYI, FORMER FORTUNE 500 CEO

Challenge

Recruit Your Personal Board of Directors

Focusing on the high trust/high value stakeholders identified in Step 1, complete your Personal Board of Directors chart. Of course, YOU are the CEO. Fill in as many seats as you can. Identify the role of each person: coach, mentor, sponsor, or ally. Then create a "Press Release" (a concise written statement that outlines your personal and professional goals) and get ready to network in Step 3.

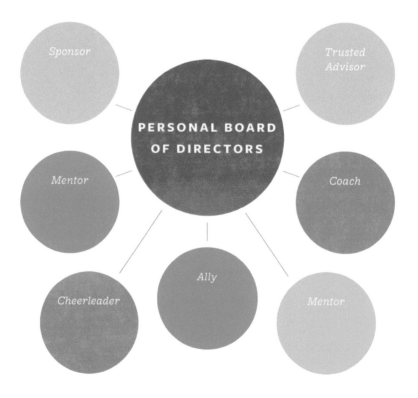

Press Release:

"Hello! I am working to assemble my Personal Board of Directors, and I would like to extend an invitation to you. Below are my top three goals for what I'd like to accomplish by establishing a personal board of directors."

(Examples: 1.) provide guidance on acquiring necessary skills and experiences, 2.) facilitate connections, 3.) share experiences and provide advice on overcoming challenges.)

1. _____

2. _____

3. _____

(P.S. You don't need to send this yet! This is just to get you in the *mood*. You will start your outreach in Step 3.)

Remember, your relationships with advisors will evolve, and you may need to distance yourself from those who hold you back or fail to recognize your growth.

Step 3:
NetWORK & Nurture

This last step takes WORK! First, network to **find** relationships, and then nurture to **grow** relationships that matter. Don't wait until you're looking for your first or next job to start networking. It takes time, so start *now*. This way, when you're ready to make a career move, you can leverage the relationship currency you've already built.

HOW TO NETWORK

I know that networking isn't easy for everyone. That's why I have capitalized the WORK in *NetWORK*. I'd like to share something that even Google doesn't know about me: I identify as an introvert. Well, okay, more likely an ambivert, which means I can turn on my social skills when necessary. I often have to present to large groups of people at LiveGirl, and I fuel up when mingling with hundreds of campers or interns. But on a Friday night, I recharge best with a quiet evening at home—with a couch, pizza, and my family (including Lucy, my dog). So yes, networking can be daunting, even for me. However, I have learned its value. I know that a networking event will likely lead to valuable connections or inspiring ideas.

Here are my networking pro tips:

- Reach out far, wide, and constantly.
- Network *through* your network. My mentee, Chioma, who is currently job hunting, went through my LinkedIn connections and asked if I could introduce her to contacts at her target companies. Smart!

- Radiate confidence: Prepare an introduction, maintain eye contact, offer a firm handshake, and smile.
- Be present: Make sure to actively listen. People appreciate when you pick up on things they've mentioned.
- Follow-up: Building a network isn't a one-and-done event! Cultivate relationships over time. Always follow up with status updates and a personalized thank you!
- Express your gratitude with a personal thank you note after every networking meeting.
- Be creative! If you *want* to meet people, you *can*. Here's a fun networking idea: engage in your community by volunteering and attending charity fundraisers to meet people.

NETWORKING ON SOCIAL MEDIA: PROCEED WITH CAUTION!

As we discussed in Chapter 1, I recommend keeping your personal social media accounts private. Use LinkedIn and other professional sites for networking, but be selective about the personal information you share. I cringe at some of the personal posts I see on LinkedIn. That said, you can strategically share professional glimpses into your personal life to allow people to know you (I occasionally post stories about how my mentees inspire me). Ultimately, while the internet is a useful tool, online connections don't necessarily translate to IRL relationships.

87%
of mentors and mentees feel empowered by their mentoring relationships and have developed greater confidence[32]

Seek Out Female Spaces

I learned the value of female affinity spaces—such as women's networks, women in leadership programs, and women's professional associations—during my tenure at GE. In my early years, the most impactful mentoring I received was through the GE Women's Network. There were significant moves (some cross-country and abroad!) that I was hesitant to make, and being coached by female mentors to lean in and take the risk was crucial for me. Taking those leaps paid off every time, especially since I had a network of female supporters. I attended the Yale Women's Leadership Executive Management Program to extend my network. It provided an incredible opportunity to interact with like-minded women from diverse backgrounds. I also belong to The WIE Suite, a membership community comprised of senior executives and founders who think beyond 'business as usual'.

I encourage you to consider joining a professional network. They serve three purposes: connection, community, and credibility. Find a network that resonates with your goals. However, it's not enough to simply join a network, you must be active! ("What you put in, you get out.") According to a study published in the Proceedings of the National Academy of Sciences (PNAS), women are more likely to land executive positions with greater authority and higher pay when they have an inner circle of close female contacts.

HOW TO NURTURE

Once you find relationships, it's time to grow and nurture them. How? By leading with authenticity and purpose. In a world where networking is often seen as transactional, standing out by genuinely connecting with others over shared values and goals can make all the difference.

Take a look at this list of positive "relationship DNA" traits outlined in Tommy Spaulding's book, *It's Not Just Who You Know*, and ask yourself how many you possess:

- Authenticity
- Confidentiality
- Curiosity
- Empathy
- Generosity
- Gratitude
- Humility
- Humor
- Vulnerability

Good news! Women tend to naturally exhibit traits that are crucial for building strong relationships. While you might feel pressured to suppress these traits in favor of more aggressive ones, I'm here to tell you that these qualities are **superpowers**. So, lead with authenticity and gratitude!

When nurturing relationships, frequency of contact is key. This means maintaining regular communication, offering support, and seeking opportunities for mutual benefit. I mentor many young women, and those who stand out are the ones who consistently stay in touch. They check in, update me on their accomplishments, and congratulate me on mine. In short, they find unique, consistent ways to stay connected. I've attached a few best practices from my mentees, Janay and Kellie, as guidance.

Dear Sheri,

A note of gratitude: Thank you so much for the opportunities you've given me! I remember being so nervous on my first official day, as this was my first internship experience, but I've grown tremendously since then. My experience as LiveGirl's social media intern was incredibly rewarding. Thank you for pushing me out of my comfort zone (into my growth zone!) to take up more space. This boosted my confidence not only at work but in life too.

It was an honor to work for you. You are a truly inspiring and passionate woman! I am excited to continue my journey through the SHE WORKS program.

I also wanted to share what I've been working on this semester. I am expanding my marketing skills by taking a photography and graphic design class. I am compiling a portfolio and am proud of my work. I will keep you posted on my future plans.

Thanks,
Janay S.

Hi Sheri,

I hope this message finds you well. I am writing to express my heartfelt gratitude for your pivotal role in shaping my professional path. Your encouragement to join SHE WORKS and be matched with an internship at Mind Money Media Inc. has profoundly impacted my career.

Here is an update: After completing my Mind Money Media Inc. internship, I transitioned to become a Production Assistant. Then, I recently accepted a full-time role as a Development Analyst Contractor at Avangrid, focusing on the renewable Offshore Wind Project for Connecticut.

When transitioning roles, I applied your coaching lessons and implemented a transition plan to ensure a seamless transition for my successor. Also, you inspired me to get involved in Avangrid's "Down to Earth Girls: An Earth Day Celebration!" organized by LiveGirl. I also recently attended a Women in Energy conference in Boston. I put my netWORKing skills to work!

Please let's catch up soon—I would love to share more about my plans and hear your advice on my next steps.

All the best,
Kellie T.

P.S. I will say, anyone who sends me a handwritten note has my heart forever! I know this is a lost art, but nothing is better than a handwritten note!

Below is a template you may use for nurturing "check-in" emails.

SUBJECT: CHECKING IN AND SHARING UPDATES

Dear [Mentor/Sponsor's Name],

I hope this email finds you well. I wanted to take a moment to check in and share some updates on my progress and experiences over the past few months.

Firstly, I want to express my gratitude for your continued support and guidance. Your insights and advice have been incredibly valuable, and I have been applying many of your suggestions in my daily work.

Here are a few highlights since our last meeting:

[Recent Achievement/Project]: I recently completed [briefly describe a project or achievement]. This experience taught me [mention any key learnings or insights], and I was reminded of the advice you gave me about [relevant advice].

[Skill Development/Training]: I have been focusing on developing my skills in [mention any skills or training]. I took [specific actions, courses, or workshops], and I am already seeing improvements in [mention specific areas of improvement].

[Networking/Relationship Building]: Following your suggestion, I have been actively working on expanding my professional network. I attended [specific event or conference] and connected with [mention any significant connections].

I would love to hear any feedback you might have, and discuss any advice for continuing to grow in these areas. If you have some time available in the coming weeks, I would appreciate the opportunity to catch up and discuss my progress in more detail.

Thank you once again for your mentorship and support. Looking forward to hearing from you soon.

Best Wishes,

ME

Now, it's time for you to put your networking skills to WORK!

Challenge

Ready, Set, Network!

Select 2-3 people from your Personal Board of Directors, then reach out and schedule/conduct a networking meeting, using some of the questions below. Be prepared so you don't waste this opportunity!

Outreach email templates:

For someone you know and feel comfortable with:

"I have an assignment from my Career Coach to conduct a career conversation. Can we schedule 15-20 minutes to connect this week or next?"

Networking through your network:

"I hope you are well. I have an assignment from my Career Coach that I am hoping you can help me with. I would love to speak with someone in [industry or job]. I was wondering if you could connect me with someone who might be helpful in this assignment. I would really appreciate it."

Cold call:

"Hello! My name is [name, title] and I have a networking assignment from my Career Coach. I admire your career and am hoping you might be willing to schedule a 20-minute mentoring call. I would appreciate learning more about your career and experiences."

Networking questions:

- Tell me about your career path and current role.
- What skills are most important to be successful at your job/role?
- How do you overcome challenges/setbacks at work?
- What is one piece of advice you would give to make [your current job position] as successful as possible?
- What are some actions an intern (or your job title) should take to show dedication and passion towards their role?
- Who else would you recommend that I network with?

Follow-up:

Sometimes you won't receive a response from your initial email, so be prepared to follow up. If you don't get a response to your follow-up email, it's okay to move on and explore other opportunities. Persistence is important, but knowing when to redirect your efforts is equally valuable. If the meeting goes well, be ready to share your "Press Release" and ask this person to serve on your Personal Board of Directors!

Gratitude:

After your networking session, be sure to follow up with a note of gratitude.

"It was great to talk with you yesterday. I am grateful to you for making time for me, and I appreciated learning about your experiences. [Add specific learning.] Thank you for encouraging me to stay in touch."

Debrief notes:

Capture the result of your networking meeting below. Replicate form on blank paper as necessary.

Name:

_____

_____

Date:

_____

_____

Topics:

_____

_____

Lessons Learned:

_____

_____

Follow-up:

_____

_____

Next Outreach Date:

_____

_____

Finding—and growing—relationships that matter will be transformative for your career. In 10, 20, 30 years you will look back and appreciate the relationships you have built and the impact they have had on your career.

AFFIRMATION

"I deserve to be surrounded by a support network that will propel me to greater heights."

Develop purpose-driven connections built on trust & shared goals

———

Identify a coach, mentor, sponsor, & ally for your support network

———

Find & grow strategic relationships that matter

09.
be an inclusive leader

"The way you make people feel is your legacy. You can either make people feel better about themselves and the world, or you can make them feel worse. You decide."

—CLEO WADE, ARTIST & AUTHOR

Be a leader who values other people's unique qualities and fosters belonging.

You've probably heard the saying, "In a world where you can be anything, be kind." Well, I'd like to suggest that we extend this sentiment to, "In a world where you can be anything, be kind **and inclusive.**" Not only will this make you a more impactful leader, but it's also the right thing to do. While the first three chapters of Part II focused on developing personal skills for career growth, this chapter addresses building inclusive leadership skills—essentially, how you make others *feel*.

Let's start by defining 'inclusive leadership'. I appreciate my mentee, Kiana White's, definition: "An inclusive leader is someone who stays curious about everyone's backgrounds and experiences, especially those different from their own. They are willing and able to learn, grow, and adapt, even when it feels uncomfortable." Inclusive leadership assures that everyone feels respected, and valued, senses that they belong, and are confident and inspired.[33] Inclusive leaders recognize that we all lead differently. Beyond the diversity of racial and ethnic backgrounds, gender identities, and sexual orientations, we must also recognize the diversity of abilities, working styles, and personalities. Consider this fact: with Gen Z in the workforce, five generations are working alongside each other, all with different styles, personalities, and approaches.

The good news is this: Gen Z is leading an **Inclusion Revolution.** Gen Z is the most diverse generation ever, and so the leadership skills required have evolved as the global workforce has shifted. But simply bringing a diverse group of people together doesn't guarantee high performance; it requires inclusive leadership. Given that only 5% of leaders globally can be defined as inclusive,[34] exemplifying inclusive leadership can distinguish you as a forward-thinking and empathetic leader, enhancing your leadership and career prospects.

To be clear, being an inclusive leader requires more than passively supporting diversity and inclusion. We are talking about being a leader who **cultivates belonging.** Diversity and inclusion expert, Verna Myers, said it best: "Diversity is being invited to the party; inclusion is being asked to dance, and belonging is dancing like no one is watching."

This chapter guides you through three steps to becoming an inclusive leader who creates spaces of belonging.

1. *Champion Inclusion*
2. *Lean Into Your Female Superpowers*
3. *Build Bridges and Diversify Your Network*

Developing inclusive leadership skills will mark you as a **rare and impactful leader** in your organization, one capable of fostering innovation, equity, and collective success.

70%

increase in likelihood of advancing in your career when you are an inclusive leader[35]

Let's start with *why* inclusive leadership is so vital. Extensive research shows us that diverse companies and teams are more innovative, productive, and profitable. Mike Robbins, author of *Bring Your Whole Self to Work: How Vulnerability Unlocks Creativity, Connection, and Performance* sums it up nicely, "When people feel they are included and belong, they can be the **best version of themselves**—and make a significant impact for themselves and the company." Makes sense!

To really understand this, let's reflect on a personal level. Likely, most of us can remember a time when we weren't included or didn't feel like we belonged.

I can recall many times during my corporate career when I was the only woman in the room. I remember an early career experience when, as the sole female auditor on my GE Audit Staff team, I sensed the team making weekend plans without me. I asked my manager if I was missing something, but he denied it. Later, I found out that the team had enjoyed a golf day, and then continued into the night at a "gentlemen's club". Not only was I excluded from the team experience, but I was also excluded from the ensuing inside jokes and "water cooler" chat. For the remainder of that assignment, I was acutely aware of my gender, and how it put me at a disadvantage.

I also want to acknowledge my own white privilege. Clearly, this discussion is more crucial for women who have been historically and systemically marginalized. Women of color report facing bias on a regular basis at work, and more than a quarter of Black women say their race has led to them missing out on an opportunity to advance.[36] (There are only two Black female CEOs in the Fortune 500.) This goes beyond feelings of exclusion to a manifestation of systemic bias that leaders need to address urgently.

Can you think of a time when you were excluded? Let this memory be your fuel as we dive into the first step!

Step 1:
Champion Inclusion

Previously, I acknowledged my white privilege. Let me go further. I have learned so much from my dear friend, Mita Mallick, bestselling author of *Reimagine Inclusion*, including this: "If you understand that you hold privilege, it is the first step in showing up as an inclusive leader."

So, let's all start by recognizing our privilege, and acknowledging that we have a lot to learn (and unlearn). The fact that you are reading this book and doing the work speaks volumes. In Chapter 5, we discussed the importance of cultivating curiosity and adopting a growth mindset. You will definitely need to put both to work here. Displaying an open mindset, along with a strong desire to understand different perspectives, is key to developing your inclusive leadership skills.

It's also important to be a visible and vocal champion by tying the importance of inclusive leadership to your *why* and talking compellingly about it. I founded LiveGirl a decade ago because I saw the need for a girls' leadership organization focused on *"building confident, inclusive leaders"* (our tagline). I wholeheartedly believe it is what our world needs most. I am in awe of how well our team models inclusive leadership and I value how we take time to appreciate our cultural differences even during staff meetings and outings. For example, at a recent team lunch, I was about to put my purse on the floor, when Shamare Holmes, our brilliant Program Director, advised me that putting your purse on the floor is considered bad luck. "A purse on the floor is money out the door," Shamare said. I laughed, put my purse on a nearby chair, and marveled at how much I always learn from her.

Here are just some of the ways that you can champion inclusion:

- Seek self-awareness on your inclusive leadership skills (see the following Challenge!).
- Educate yourself and learn about cultural differences.
- Advocate for inclusive policies and practices within your organization.
- Lead by example by valuing and respecting all team members, ensuring everyone has a voice, and creating space for marginalized voices.

Challenge

Strengthen Your Inclusive Leadership Muscle

The goal of this challenge is to arm you with self-knowledge so you can focus your energies in the right place. First, take a look at the **Six Cs of Inclusive Leadership by Deloitte.**[37] Then take inventory of your biases, strengths, and areas for improvement.

Commitment: Demonstrating a deep personal commitment to diversity and inclusion, driving accountability and sustained efforts towards creating an inclusive environment.

Courage: Showing the bravery to challenge the status quo, address biases, and speak up for inclusion even when it's uncomfortable.

Cognizance of Bias: Being aware of personal and organizational biases, and actively working to mitigate their impact on decision-making processes.

Curiosity: Displaying an open mindset and a strong desire to understand different perspectives, fostering a culture of continuous learning and openness.

Cultural Intelligence: Understanding and respecting cultural differences, enabling effective interactions and collaborations across diverse groups.

Collaboration: Creating a team environment that values diverse contributions and encourages the sharing of ideas and perspectives to achieve collective success.

1. **Reflect: Which of these traits resonate with you most and why?**

   _____

2. Identify and circle the traits you believe to be your strengths.

   _____

3. Now identify at least one trait you need to grow and develop further. Identify an Implementation Intention below. (You learned these in Chapter 2!)

   _____

Example:

Trait:

Cultural Intelligence

Implementation Intention:

I will take a Cultural Intelligence (CQ) Assessment [behavior] by December 15 [time] online @ HBR [location].
I will also read The Culture Map *by Erin Meyer [behavior] by December 15 [time] at the library [location].*

Trait:

   _____

Implementation Intention:

I will _____ at _____ in _____ .
      [behavior]   *[time]*   *[location]*

4. Bonus step: Seek feedback from others on whether you are perceived as inclusive, especially from people who are different from you.

The Importance of Allies by Ruth-Ann Bucknor

———

(LIVEGIRL SHINE ON SCHOLAR)

"As an African American woman in the workforce, I am no stranger to the subtle yet pervasive microaggressions that women of color face on a daily basis. Often, I am met with the backhanded compliment, "You speak so well," as if eloquence is unexpected from someone like me. My ideas are frequently dismissed or ignored until a colleague repeats them, at which point they are suddenly deemed valuable. When I assert myself, I am labeled as "aggressive" or "intimidating," descriptors that contrast starkly with the "assertive" or "strong leader" labels given to my non-minority counterparts for the same behavior.

Comments on my hair, whether it's styled naturally or otherwise, subtly suggest that my natural features are unprofessional or out of place in a corporate setting. These experiences are not unique to me but are shared by many women of color. They highlight the critical need for leaders who are willing to challenge these biases, advocate for genuine inclusion, and foster a workplace culture that respects and values our diverse contributions. Allies can amplify our voices, confront microaggressions head-on, and help create an environment where everyone can thrive authentically."

Step 2:
Lean Into Your
Female Superpowers

By 'female superpowers', I mean 'empathy' and 'emotional intelligence'. Let's start with some simple definitions so we're on the same page.

EMPATHY: Understanding and sharing the feelings of others.
EMOTIONAL INTELLIGENCE: Being aware of one's own emotions and those of others, and using this awareness to guide decisions.

According to extensive research by inclusive leadership expert, Dr. Shirley Davis, these traits align with what employees seek in a manager. Let's test this. Close your eyes and think about the best manager you've had. *What specific actions or traits did they have that made you feel supported and valued?*

Now, how would you describe their leadership traits?

Likely, they led with empathy and emotional intelligence. Let's dive deeper into why these traits are so important and how you can cultivate them in your leadership journey.

EMPATHY

Honestly, ladies, we've got this! According to Korn Ferry research, **women are 45% more likely than men to demonstrate empathy.** In other words, leading with empathy is a female superpower! Even still, I see many young women leaning away from their female superpowers, because they have been conditioned to think that effective leadership traits align with what they see—predominantly white men. That's because there is a **visibility gap for female role models.**

But rest assured, science and our culture are catching up. During the pandemic, much was written about the success of countries with female leaders who led with empathy. One exemplar was New Zealand's Prime Minister, Jacinda Ardern, who received global praise for her empathetic communication and swift, decisive actions, resulting in low infection and mortality rates. Other examples included Germany, Taiwan, Iceland, and Finland.

Also, new studies have shown that companies with more women in leadership roles often outperform their peers financially. This is attributed to the leadership traits women commonly exhibit, such as empathy and emotional intelligence.[38] So, the message here is to **lean into your female superpowers!** Dismiss the misinformed gender tropes that women are too soft and emotional. Continue to do what you do best—listening actively and empathetically to your team members, and valuing their unique perspectives and experiences.

EMOTIONAL INTELLIGENCE (EQ)

Emotional intelligence (often referred to as EQ), is an individual's ability to understand and manage their own emotions, as well as recognize and influence the emotions of others. "A person with high emotional intelligence can grasp what makes us human, whilst simultaneously recognizing what makes us different from one another."[39] This skill allows us to value diverse perspectives, and create an environment where everyone feels respected and heard. According to Korn Ferry research, **women score higher than men on nearly all emotional intelligence competencies,** except emotional self-control, where no gender differences are observed. Nice!

I have found this to be true in my career. I have worked with some brilliant people who lacked emotional intelligence, and I observed that their impact was limited because of it. Of course, we all have moments where we are overcome by strong emotions: anger, fear, and frustration. It's how we handle these emotions that matter. Each of us needs to devise personal techniques when we feel an emotional storm brewing. My approach? I visualize putting my feelings into an 'emotional intelligence box'. Then I get curious, and ask myself, "**What** am I feeling" and "**Why** am I feeling this way?" I breathe slowly and picture myself on the outside looking into the box, like a social anthropologist. When the answer appears, I make sure to practice self-compassion. "Ahhhh! Now I know why this feeling is here. I see you." Validating your emotions is often the best way to move forward. Now you are best suited to determine how you might grow from this situation.

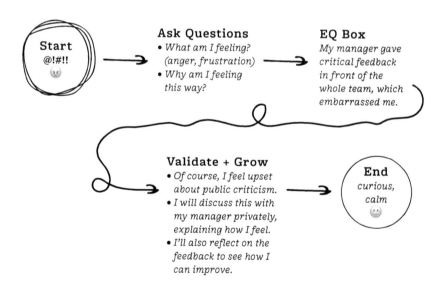

71%
of employers
value emotional
intelligence more
than technical skills
when evaluating
candidates[40]

Challenge

Develop a Daily Empathy Practice

Journaling is a great way to build your empathy and emotional intelligence. Reflecting on personal experiences, and consciously adopting different perspectives, can offer meaningful insights. Try it here, and adapt going forward in a blank journal.

Today's Self-Reflection

- **Your Experience:** What happened? Include as many details as possible.
- **Your Emotional Response:** How did you feel during this event? Identify and describe your emotions.
- **Your Thoughts and Beliefs:** What were you thinking at the time? What beliefs or assumptions did you have?
- **Actions Taken:** What did you do in response to this event?

_____

_____

_____

_____

_____

_____

_____

_____

_____

_____

Flip the Script

Choose one significant event from today to explore further. Reflect on the other person's perspective by writing about:

- **Their Experience:** What might the other person have experienced during this event? Describe it from their point of view.
- **Their Emotions:** How might they have felt? Identify possible emotions they experienced.
- **Their Thoughts and Beliefs:** What might they have been thinking? What beliefs or assumptions could they have held?
- **Their Actions**: Why do you think they acted the way they did? Consider their motivations and intentions.

_____

_____

_____

_____

_____

_____

_____

_____

_____

_____

Now, reflect on how you will apply this empathy going forward. Continue this as a daily practice to build self-awareness and empathy.

Step 3:
Build Bridges and Diversify Your Network

A few years ago I was interviewing Mita Mallick and she said something that resonated with me: "Inclusive leaders build authentic bridges to people whose lives are different from their own." Mita was talking about the importance of cultivating relationships with people from diverse backgrounds and creating an environment where everyone feels valued and included.

I grew up in a small, homogenous town (like so many American midwestern towns). Back then, I honestly didn't give much thought to diversity and inclusion, and I certainly didn't understand how it applied to me. When I attended Michigan State University (student population: 50,000+), along with two of my best hometown friends, we agreed to accept random roommate assignments to "fly" and meet new people. (We also agreed to nurture our relationship by scheduling a monthly night out, and are still friends to this day! Ya-Ya sisters!)

I was matched with Nancy Bailey, a college sophomore who was very different from me. I grew up on a farm, while Nancy hailed from urban Detroit. I was an ambivert ready to party on a Friday night, while Nancy was an introvert who preferred reading a book. Importantly, I was white, and Nancy was Black. Nancy quickly and generously introduced me to her friends, expanding my world. She was intrigued (and a little amused) by my music and food choices, and she shared hers. She made me question and reflect upon my protected upbringing, and I became a bigger and better person because of Nancy. Most importantly, as I reflect, Nancy taught me to be open-minded and curious about differences.

Nancy and I haven't stayed in touch, but if she is reading this, I want her to know how much she influenced the inclusive person I am today. Every time I meet someone different and new, it expands my worldview.

Inclusive leaders can build strong, diverse networks, which leads to enhanced reputation and greater opportunities for career growth. Consider this fact: Inclusive leaders are **2.3 times more likely to have strong professional relationships** and networks.[41] The next challenge will help you build this skill.

Challenge

Expand Your Circle of Trust

This exercise[42] will focus on your 'inner circle', encouraging self-aware-ness as you explore how diverse—or not—it is. It's a helpful tool for uncovering unconscious and affinity bias, and encouraging more inclusive networking practices.

First, identify six of your "go-to" people at work/school/another group. Think of them as your inner circle—the people you consider trustworthy, and whose counsel you seek when making decisions. Write their names in the first column.

Name	Gender	Sexual Orientation	Race / Ethnicity	Age	Education Level	Nationality	Ableness	Native Language

Now, place a checkmark in the columns where you share the same identity. For example, if you both identify as female, place a checkmark in the gender column. Continue for all columns. When finished, reflect on the outcome.

- How diverse is your circle of trust?
- How might you diversify your inner circle of confidants?

Don't be surprised if you find that your circle of trust is homoge-nous. Consider this fact: 75% of white Americans have entirely white social networks. Likewise, 65% of Black Americans report having an all-Black social network.[43] In fact, according to Hyper Island, "Our closest advisors and those we rely on most for sound insight are often an unconscious mirror of ourselves."

It takes work and intention to diversify your network, but I promise, the outcome is worth it! Building diverse friendships can break down stereotypes and increase empathy across different racial and ethnic groups. Here are three ways to build a more diverse and inclusive professional network, enhancing your career growth and perspective:

1. Join diverse professional associations: e.g., join Paradigm for Parity or a similar organization
2. Attend diverse networking events: e.g., attend a Juneteenth celebration or an AAPI or LGBTQ+ networking event
3. Deliberately seek out different experiences: e.g., search for opportunities to work with cross-functional or multi-disciplinary teams

These steps will help you, as Simone E. Morris, author of *52 Tips for Owning Your Career: Practical Advice For Career Success*, recommends: "Build your inclusion muscles by putting yourself in scenarios that increase your cultural competency."

"Why be a star when you can make a constellation?"

—MARIAME KABA, WRITER

Finally, remember that inclusive leadership is **not** about occasional grand gestures, but everyday, smaller-scale comments and actions. It is a lifestyle, and you must **live the values.** I hope you view this chapter as the beginning of your inclusive leadership journey. I am still learning too, and I have included some resources on my website (SheriWestLeadership.com) for those who would like to further their journey.

AFFIRMATION

"I will create a welcoming space where everyone feels valued and heard."

*Seek self-awareness
& create space for
marginalized voices*

———

*Lead with your female
superpowers: empathy &
emotional intelligence*

———

*Expand your inner circle
& cultivate diverse
relationships*

10.
feed your genius

"And the day came when the risk to remain tight in a bud was more painful than the risk it took to blossom."

—ANAÏS NIN, WRITER

Build habits that prioritize wellness and balance.

Congratulations! You've completed the first nine chapters, which will help you **grow** as a leader. This final chapter focuses on skills that will help you **thrive** as a leader. This means continuously growing, feeling fulfilled, and maintaining a healthy work-life integration.

Here's where I truly think my age (aka wisdom!) comes into play. What I really want you to know is this: You are wildly talented with limitless potential **and** you face a scary, bumpy, road ahead. So, it's vital that you develop foundational habits and skills to continuously "feed your genius" and sustain yourself.

After all, **we must first lead ourselves before we can lead others.** And a key part of leading ourselves is instilling good habits, and nurturing joy and gratitude daily.

Here are three steps to feed your genius and thrive in the long term:

1. *Design Your Day*
2. *Commit to Growing*
3. *Rest & Refuel*

These lessons will enhance your productivity while maintaining the energy and resilience required for you to thrive throughout your career.

Full confession: I've learned these lessons the hard way. Since my first job at age ten, working on a strawberry farm, I've always been running from one challenge to the next. To be honest, I have a complicated relationship with what it takes for me to feel productive—and I often feel "unproductive" (whatever that means!) when taking time off. After the birth of my third child, I experienced burnout. (More on this later.)

I've had two major reckonings about living and working with balance and intention. The first came when I became a manager and realized that, to be a good leader, I needed to model and coach my team on efficiency and wellness. Then, after having kids, I understood that working relentlessly around the clock was no longer possible—I needed better work-life integration. As my three kids grew into brilliant, observant individuals, I saw how closely they were watching me. I realized that many of my habits would become their habits, making it more important than ever to live with intention and purpose.

I adopted the mantra **"work smarter, not harder"** to achieve my ambitious goals while prioritizing my family and wellness. I committed to **showing myself grace** when things didn't go perfectly. I learned that I could work less **and** be more productive—and model this behavior for others.

So, guided by my experience, let's get into the first step that will help you thrive as you advance in your career and life.

Step 1:
Design Your Day

The first step is to understand that YOU are the architect of your day, your week, your year, and your life. So, how will you choose to live it? Here's a tip: Apply discipline to control your day, rather than respond to it. Once you design your day with purpose, you will see your dreams materialize.

There is a saying, "Pay attention to what you pay attention to." It emphasizes the importance of being mindful of where you focus your attention. We must all adopt practices that work for us. At 54 years old, I have tried many practices, wandered away from some, and returned to others. But the key is to design your day with practices *that work for you.* For me, I aim to incorporate these two key principles daily:

Start each day with focus: I have found it essential to be intentional about my morning routine. In the past, I have had periods where I'm beholden to other people's needs from the moment I open my eyes. Now, I start my day with focus. Upon waking, I practice a series of daily rituals, including a morning meditation, reading, and exercising. I read or listen to the *Morning Brew* and NPR's *Up First,* which keep me informed and inspired. Yes, it means setting my alarm a bit earlier, but it is worth it. Then, I begin my work day with a quick goal-setting and planning session—intending to control my day, versus responding to it.

Focus on the good: I believe in the power of positive psychology and incorporate a daily gratitude practice. This can be quick and simple. I typically journal and write down three things I am grateful for that day, and at least one thing I did right. For example, my daily gratitudes may include: 1.) my mom receiving a clear PET scan, 2.) a generous donor making a high school retreat possible, and 3.) a sunny walk with my adorable Goldendoodle, Lucy. While gratitude is focused on celebrating things *outside of myself* (to stay connected to the bigger picture), I also take the time to express gratitude *towards myself*. This is called an *appreciation practice*. For this, I ask "What did I do right today?" I force myself to identify at least one thing to appreciate about myself—even if it is the type of day described in my favorite children's book *Alexander and the Terrible, Horrible, No Good, Very Bad Day* by Judith Viorst. It might be how I handled a difficult situation, or how I regulated my emotions by not immediately responding to a frustrating email. These aren't the headlines that front a resume or LinkedIn post, but rather the small daily, positive steps that will help you realize the cumulative effect of your actions. This practice will also encourage you to stop waiting for external validation, as you come to more regularly celebrate yourself.

The power of positive psychology:

If you believe it will work out, you will see opportunities.

If you believe it won't, you will see obstacles.

Practice a mini-reflection now, and identify three gratitudes and one appreciation.

Challenge

Be the Architect of Your Day

Put it all together and design a daily routine that **feels good** and results in **good outcomes.** For this challenge, I will first provide my daily design as an inspiration of sorts, and then task you with evaluating your current schedule and designing your optimal day.

Week Day

Early Morning Block:
- Walk my beloved Goldendoodle, Lucy, enjoy a steaming cup of coffee, journal
- Family care, "feed my genius," read news
- 45-minute Pilates

Morning Block
- In office, two-hour block for strategic thinking, problem-solving, writing, etc. (most important tasks of the day)
- Work Flow

Afternoon Block
- Work Flow
- Respond to emails

Evening Block
- Family care (dinner, phone calls)
- Reading
- Gratitude & Appreciation Practice *"What did I do right today?"*

Now, it's your turn to design your day.

First, reflect and identify any daily practices that are currently not serving you. This could include scrolling on social media, letting your inbox control your day, or spending too much time on low-priority tasks.

Week Day
Early Morning Block

_____

_____

Morning Block

_____

_____

Afternoon Block

_____

_____

Evening Block

_____

_____

Weekend

For the optimal weekend day, first identify what is energizing and uplifting to you, and then plan a joyful "dream" day filled with those activities.

_____

_____

Remember that every day is a choice. You "get" to go to class, work, etc. Be empowered by your choices.

Step 2: Commit to Growing

My hope for you is that you **never** stop growing. (May the flowers in this book be a reminder to keep blooming and growing!) I wrote earlier about how the world is constantly evolving. Just think how different your life was five years ago pre-pandemic. In Chapter 3, we discussed the importance of adopting a growth mindset to learn and grow continuously. This mindset will help you become a lifelong learner, finding joy in challenging yourself to acquire new skills, technologies, and more. If you do, you'll continue to blossom with increased confidence, resilience, and adaptability.

I learned this from my mom, who was a teacher. (P.S. I believe teaching—shaping future minds—to be one of the most noble and important professions in our universe!) Thanks to her, I have always valued and sought education. As my close friends and LiveGirl staff can attest, I am an avid reader. I am always carrying and recommending books. (Veronica DeLandro, LiveGirl's extraordinary Executive Director, laughingly calls it "Sheri's Book Club".) But in fact, research shows that, while less successful people read mostly for entertainment, those at the top are avid readers of self-improvement books. 85% of successful people read two or more educational books per month.[44]

Like any skill, this one needs practice and intention. To become an avid reader, I recommend using an app like Goodreads. I love how you can mark your books "read" and identify the books you "want to read". Goodreads also allows you to set a reading challenge and track your progress for accountability. My husband and I apply a little positive peer pressure and challenge each other. We both aim to read 50 books per year and make it a friendly competition. (I typically alternate fiction and nonfiction books.) You can also "friend" others to view their reading list and recommendations. If you decide to join Goodreads, please friend me!

It's important to adopt a mindset that encourages you to seek and integrate continuous learning into your life. Here are some fun activities to try:

- Complete an online course.
- Attend a webinar or virtual workshop.
- Join a professional organization.
- Listen to a podcast episode relevant to your career.
- Write a summary of a research article.
- Network with a new professional contact on LinkedIn.
- Ask for feedback from a mentor or supervisor.
- Participate in a discussion in an online forum or group.
- Practice a new skill related to your job.

30%

of executives say
'willingness to learn'
is the characteristic
they consider
most necessary
to succeed[45]

Challenge

Enroll in *Confidence Unleashed U*

Time for another choose-your-own adventure challenge! Select an option below.

Become AI Savvy:

Generative AI's (gen AI) implications on the workforce and your future are significant. A McKinsey analysis estimates that gen AI could add between 2.6 and 4.4 trillion annually to the global economy. You can add value to your job skills by learning how to use gen AI platforms.

For this challenge, you will learn more about AI through a series of "scavenger hunt" tasks that cover various aspects of AI, including its history, applications, ethical considerations, and practical hands-on experiences.

- **History and Basics:** Find and summarize a short article about the history of AI. What are the key milestones?
- **AI in Daily Life:** Identify five everyday applications of AI (e.g., virtual assistants, recommendation systems, prepping for job interviews, etc.).
- **Hands-On Experience:** Complete a basic AI tutorial on platforms like Codecademy, Coursera, or Google's AI Experiments.
- **Ethics in AI:** Watch a TED Talk or read an article about the ethical considerations in AI and write a brief reflection.

- **AI Tools:** Explore and use a simple AI tool or app, such as a ChatGPT or image recognition app, and describe your experience.
- **Career Insights:** Find an interview with an AI professional and note down three pieces of advice they give to newcomers in the field.

Stay Fresh: Dive into a New Book or Enroll in an Online Course
As discussed, becoming an avid reader is an important part of becoming a continuous learner. So, for this challenge, pick a book or an online course—from my favorites list below, or from your own list. Give yourself two weeks to finish the book or course.

- *Dare to Lead* by Brené Brown
- *Lead to Win: How to Be a Powerful, Impactful, Influential Leader in Any Environment* by Carla A. Harris
- *Lead from the Outside* by Stacey Abrams
- *Myth of the Nice Girl* by Fran Hauser
- *My Own Words* by Ruth Bader Ginsburg
- *Think Again* by Adam Grant
- *Power Moves* by Lauren McGoodwin
- *Reimagine Inclusion* by Mita Mallick
- *The Connection Cure* by Julia Hotz
- LinkedIn Learning: Skills for Advancing as a Woman in Leadership
- Other _____

Once completed, answer these prompts:

1. How did the concepts or strategies presented in the book or course challenge your existing beliefs about leadership?

   _____

   _____

   _____

   _____

   _____

2. Which part of the book resonated most with you, and why?

   _____

   _____

   _____

   _____

   _____

3. What specific actions or changes will you implement in your daily work or leadership style based on the book's recommendations?

   _____

   _____

   _____

   _____

   _____

Step 3:
Rest & Refuel

I'll be honest. Mid-career, I let my gas tank run empty. After the birth of my third child, I experienced burnout. I realized that I was not successfully integrating my work and family life. (A term I'd like to banish is "work-life balance," because there are times when you will not feel balanced at all. For this reason, I prefer the term "integration.") So, I decided to take a career pause. During this time, I strove to reconnect with self-care, joy, and gratitude, and I am happy to share some of the principles that have since shaped my daily life. These principles are informed by knowing and honoring your limits.

Set boundaries: Setting healthy boundaries is crucial in our increasingly remote 24/7 world. Here are a few common boundary breakers that we've all likely allowed in the past:

- *Checking your work email outside of office hours.*
- *Making yourself available on Slack 24/7—to solve any problem that might arise.*
- *Picking up work outside of your job description at a moment's notice.*

It is important to set both physical and emotional boundaries. In Dr. Dana Gionta's book, *From Stressed to Centered*, she offers a step-by-step process for assessing personal boundaries at work:

- Know your limits.
- Pay attention to your feelings.
- Give yourself permission to set boundaries.
- Consider your environment.

Here are a few examples of boundaries that I have set:

- *Don't respond to emails after 6pm or on weekends.*
- *Decline unnecessary meetings (including any recurring meetings that have failed to produce value); question any meeting length > 30 minutes.*
- *Set an OOO message when in deep work mode or on personal days.*
- *The day(s) after a big event or deliverable, I block "rest and reflect" time on my calendar.*

When setting boundaries, listen to the **dread in your head**. Dread is an important emotion, defined as "a strong feeling of fear or anxiety about something that may happen in the future." What do you feel dread about? Examples include upcoming deadlines, overwhelming responsibilities, committee meetings, difficult relationships, public speaking, or performance reviews. Chances are, you need to set boundaries where/when you feel dread.

"Marie Kondo" your social media feed: For many, social media has a negative effect on self-esteem. So, my advice is to curate a feed that inspires you. Unfollow anyone that feeds you negative vibes. It's that easy! (Marie Kondo is a renowned Japanese organizing consultant and author, best known for her KonMari method, which advocates decluttering and organizing possessions based on sparking joy.) You may also choose to do a digital detox and remove yourself completely from social media for periods of time. Your social media should spark joy! So, if it is causing dread instead, it's time to revisit the way you interact with it.

Show yourself kindness: I use positive affirmations to guide me forward. At LiveGirl, we start all of our programs with the affirmation, "I am smart. I am strong. I am special." Whatever affirmation resonates with you, use it as a daily personal power mantra to fuel you forward. Always show yourself kindness. I hope you have been saying the end-of-chapter affirmations aloud! Pick your favorite and keep saying it daily.

Rest: Sometimes you just need rest. It's okay to take a personal mental health day. Let me repeat: It is okay not to be okay! Taking time off may even give you the perspective and space to dream up beautiful new things. Also, sometimes it will be necessary for you to take time away, or disengage in relationships or activities to protect your peace. Again, IT IS OKAY. The only person you owe in this world is YOU.

Finally, remember to practice self-compassion when framing your need for the above by applying the **power of "and"**...

- You can set boundaries **and** be kind.
- You can work less **and** be more productive.
- You can be strong **and** need rest/support.

As the singer, Lizzo, says, "You are a work in progress **and** a masterpiece at the same damn time."

The bottom line is that it's okay to feel stressed, burned out, or overwhelmed. Find what helps you unwind, whether it is meditation, music, poetry, or a moment of quiet. (P.S. spending time in nature or near water has been shown to have relaxing and stress-reducing effects.) Whatever it is, always prioritize your self-care.

34%
of women are
almost always
burned out[46]

Beat the Burnout

Burnout refers to a state of physical and emotional exhaustion, often resulting from prolonged stress and overwork. It is characterized by feelings of persistent fatigue, cynicism, and a sense of reduced professional efficacy. Women are particularly prone to burnout due to the challenges of balancing multiple roles, workplace inequities, and cultural expectations. For me, balancing a career and children was overwhelming. On top of that, we relocated frequently with our careers (my three children were born in three different states!), which left me without a support system. Unfortunately, for women, our societal norms emphasize self-sacrifice over self-care. But you have the power to change that. Importantly, you must first possess the self-awareness to identify burnout. Here are four "Red Flag questions" that will determine if you are burned out:

1. Do I often feel physically and emotionally exhausted?
2. Do I feel detached or cynical about my work or personal responsibilities?
3. Am I experiencing a decline in my productivity and effectiveness at work?
4. Have I lost interest in activities that I once found enjoyable or fulfilling?

If you answered "yes" to any of these questions, take the prospect of burnout seriously, and follow the suggestions in this chapter.

Challenge

Align with Your "To Feel List"

Often, our capitalist culture ties self-worth to output. Hence, we all maintain endless "To Do" lists, and are guided by a sense of hyper-productivity, e.g., *How many checkmarks can I get today?!* To step away from this line of thinking, reframe and focus on how you want to feel, as well as what you want to accomplish. I call this my "To Feel List".

First, think about how you want to **feel** in various aspects of your life (e.g., at work, in relationships, in personal growth). This may change over time. For example, as I write this and head into the summer season, I want to feel rested, fulfilled, and nurtured by family and friends.

Next, write down activities, habits, or actions that will help you achieve these feelings. For me, it is taking time off to refuel, read, write, and spend time with family and friends.

My "To Feel List"

How I want to feel:

_____

_____

_____

_____

_____

_____

_____

_____

These activities, habits, or actions will help me achieve these feelings:

_____

_____

_____

_____

_____

The one new boundary I will set to protect my peace:

_____

_____

_____

_____

_____

My Affirmation (Personal Power Mantra):

_____

_____

_____

_____

_____

Regularly review and update your list, integrating activities that foster these feelings into your daily routine.

"Almost everything will work again if you unplug it for a few minutes, including you."

—ANNE LAMOTT, WRITER & ACTIVIST

Congratulations! You've made it to the end of this book. We had some fun, right?! Remember, **the power is inside of you** to grow and rise as a leader. Please heed my call to "work smarter, not harder" to achieve your ambitious goals **while** prioritizing your wellness. The world needs you to keep shining.

I started the book by saying, "I believe in you." Now, it's time to **believe in yourself** and put the mindset and skills you've developed to work, unleashing your confidence and growing into the leader you were born to be. *What are you waiting for?* You are truly a marvel. **The future is yours!**

PS. I would love to hear from you! Your stories and feedback are important. Please share and tag me on LinkedIn or email Sheri@ Confidence-Unleashed.com. If you found this book helpful, please share it with others!

AFFIRMATION

"I am a marvel, embracing confidence & grace as I prioritize my wellness."

*Be the architect
of your day & live
with intention*

———

*Adopt a continuous
growth mindset*

———

*Honor your limits;
rest & refuel as needed*

ENDNOTES

1 Henry Chiang Samrudhi Kaulapure Daniel J. Sandberg, PhD, CFA, "Elusive Parity: Key Gender Parity Metric Falls for First Time in 2 Decades", *S&P Global*, Mar. 8, 2024, https://www.spglobal.com/marketintelligence/en/news-insights/research/elusive-parity-key-gender-parity-metric-falls-for-first-time-in-2-decades

2 Emily Field, Alexis Krivkovich, Sandra Kügele, Nicole Robinson, and Lareina Yee, "Women in the Workplace 2023 Report", McKinsey & Company in partnership with Lean In, Oct. 5, 2023

3 Sunil Solanki, "The Power of Personal Branding in Business and Professional Growth", *LinkedIn: The Marketing Roadmap,* July 9, 2023

4 YPulse, Gen Z's Top 50 Most Authentic Brands / 2023, https://www.ypulse.com/authentic-brands-2023/

5 Susan McPherson, "How Much of Your "Authentic Self" Should You Really Bring to Work?", *Harvard Business Review*, Feb. 12, 2021

6 Geoffrey Scott, CPRW, "30+ Essential Resume Statistics in 2024—Analysis of 25,000 Job Applications", Feb. 1, 2024, https://resumegenius.com/blog/resume-help/resume-statistics

7 Gettysburg College, "One Third of Your Life Is Spent At Work", accessed Jun. 25, 2024, https://www.gettysburg.edu/news/stories

8 McKinsey & Company, "Help your employees find purpose—or watch them leave", accessed July 25, 2024. https://www.mckinsey.com/featured-insights/future-of-work/help-your-employees-find-purpose-or-watch-them-leave

9 Barrett Wissman, "An Accountability Partner Makes You Vastly More Likely to Succeed," *Entrepreneur*, Mar. 20, 2018 (Study originally published by The American Society of Training and Development in 2014)

10 Luciana Paulise, "75% Of Women Executives Experience Imposter Syndrome In The Workplace", *Forbes*, Mar. 8, 2023 (Originally published by KPMG Women's Leadership Study in 2015)

11 Anna Bahney, "Best Way For Women To Advance At Work? Leave The Comfort Zone Behind", *Forbes*, Feb. 17, 2015

12 Vitale Buford Hardin, "Perfectionism Research", Vitale & Company, accessed Nov. 1, 2023, https://vitaleandco.com/perfectionism-research/

13 Barna, "New Data on Gen Z—Perceptions of Pressure, Anxiety and Empowerment", Jan. 28, 2021, https://www.barna.com/research/gen-z-success/

14 Dove Self-Esteem Project, accessed Dec. 1, 2023, https://www.dove.com/us/en/stories/about-dove/dove-self-esteem-project.html

15 Luciana Paulise, "75% Of Women Executives Experience Imposter Syndrome In The Workplace", *Forbes* (Original study by KPMG), Mar. 8, 2023, https://www.forbes.com/sites/lucianapaulise/2023/03/08/75-of-women-executives-experience-imposter-syndrome-in-the-workplace/

16 Kaila Kea-Lewis, "Why 60% Qualified Is Enough, According to a Recruiter", InHerSight, accessed Jun. 25, 2024, www.inhersight.com

17 Linda A. Hill, Ann Le Cam, Sunand Menon, and Emily Tedards, "Curiosity, Not Coding: 6 Skills Leaders Need in the Digital Age," *Harvard Business School*, Feb. 14, 2022, https://hbswk.hbs.edu/item/six-unexpected-traits-leaders-need-in-the-digital-era

18 American Psychological Association, "2023 Work in America Survey", accessed Jun. 25, 2024, https://www.apa.org/pubs/reports/work-in-america/2023-workplace-health-well-being

19 Taylor Borden, "Career Breaks Are Different For Women—Here's What Happens When They Come Back", *LinkedIn News: The Work Shift*, Feb. 29, 2024

20 Michel J. Dugas and Robert Ladouceur, "The Role of Intolerance of Uncertainty", APA PsycNet, accessed Jan. 1, 2024, https://psycnet.apa.org/record/2004-16375-006

21 Robert B. (Rob) Kaiser, Ryne A. Sherman, and Robert Hogan, "It Takes Versatility to Lead in a Volatile World", *Harvard Business Review*, Mar. 7, 2023

22 Francesca Gino, "The Business Case for Curiosity," *Harvard Business Review Magazine*, September-October 2018

23 Francesca Gino, "The Business Case for Curiosity," *Harvard Business Review Magazine*, September-October 2018

24 Sallie Krawcheck, *Own It: The Power of Women at Work,* (New York: Crown Business, 2017)

25 J. Maureen Henderson, "When It Comes To Internships, Connections Matter Most", *Forbes,* Jun. 30, 2017, https://www.forbes.com/sites/jmaureenhenderson/2017/06/30/when-it-comes-to-internships-connections-matter-most/

26 Simone E. Morris, *52 Tips for Owning Your Career: Practical Advice For Career Success,* page 121

27 National Association of Colleges and Employers Job Outlook 2024, accessed Feb. 1, 2024, https://www.naceweb.org/docs/default-source/default-document-library/2023/publication/research-report/2024-nace-job-outlook.pdf

28 Joseph G. Hadfield, "Women Speak Up Less When They're Outnumbered", *BYU Magazine,* Winter 2013 Issue

29 Lean In, "Women in the Workplace Study 2023", Lean In, accessed Feb. 1, 2024, https://leanin.org/women-in-the-workplace

30 Bates Communications, "Executive Presence: A Model of Highly Effective Leadership" 2021, (Original study by Center for Talent Innovation)

31 Chief, "The Network Effect", *Chief Networking Study,* July 19, 2023, https://join.chief.com/rs/702-CII-507/images/Chief%20Networking%20Study.pdf

32 Grace Winstanely, "Mentoring Statistics You Need To Know – 2024", MentorLoop, Feb. 21, 2024, https://mentorloop.com/blog/mentoring-statistics/

33 *Harvard Business Review,* "The Key to Inclusive Leadership", accessed July 25, 2024. https://store.hbr.org/product/the-key-to-inclusive-leadership/H05GLB

34 Korn Ferry, "The Benefits of Inclusive Leadership", Korn Ferry Insights, accessed Mar. 2024, https://www.kornferry.com/insights/featured-topics/diversity-equity-inclusion/the-benefits-of-inclusive-leadership

35 Dnika j. Travis, PhD, Emily Shaffer, PhD, Jennifer Thorpe-Moscon, PhD, "Getting Real About Inclusive Leadership: Why Change Starts With You", Catalyst, accessed Mar. 1, 2024, https://www.catalyst.org/wp-content/uploads/2020/03/Getting-Real-About-Inclusive-Leadership-Report-2020update.pdf

36 Lean In, "Women in the Workplace: Black Women", *Lean In,* accessed Mar. 1, 2024, https://leanin.org/article/women-in-the-workplace-black-women

37 Deloitte, "Six Signature Traits of Inclusive Leadership", accessed Jan. 25, 2024. https://www2.deloitte.com/us/en/insights/topics/talent/six-signature-traits-of-inclusive-leadership.html

38 Jack Zenger and Joseph Folkman, "Research: Women Score Higher Than Men in Most Leadership Skills", *Harvard Business Review,* Jun. 25, 2019, https://hbr.org/2019/06/research-women-score-higher-than-men-in-most-leadership-skills

39 Lauren Landry, "Why Emotional Intelligence Is Important In Leadership', *Harvard Business Review,* Apr. 3, 2019

40 Lauren Landry, "Why Emotional Intelligence Is Important In Leadership', *Harvard Business Review,* Apr. 3, 201

41 Juliette Bourke, Bernadette Dillon, "The Diversity & Inclusion Revolution", *Deloitte Review,* Issue 22, Jan. 2018

42 Hyper Island Toolbox, "Circle of Trust Exercise", accessed Feb. 2015 from https://toolbox.hyperisland.com/the-circle-of-trust-unconscious-bias

43 Public Religion Research Institute, "American Bubbles: Perceptions of Racial, Ethnic, and Religious Diversity", accessed Mar. 2024 from https://www.prri.org/research/american-bubbles-perceptions-of-racial-ethnic-and-religious-diversity/

44 Sandy Clarke, "How The Power Of Reading Holds The Key To Success", Leaderonomics, Jun. 22, 2017, https://www.leaderonomics.com/articles/personal/power-of-reading-and-success

45 Caroline Castrillon, "Why A Growth Mindset Is Essential For Career Success", *Forbes,* Dec. 10, 2021, https://www.forbes.com/sites/carolinecastrillon/2019/07/09/why-a-growth-mindset-is-essential-for-career-success/

46 Lydia Saad, Sangeeta Agrawal and Ben Wigert, "Gender Gap in Worker Burnout Widened Amid the Pandemic", *Gallup,* Dec. 27, 2021, https://www.gallup.com/workplace/358349/gender-gap-worker-burnout-widened-amid-pandemic.aspx

"Nothing in nature blooms all year long, so don't expect yourself to do so either."

— UNKNOWN

How lucky am I? Over the years, I have built an incredible village and support system that lifts me up at every turn. I am deeply grateful to everyone in my village, especially:

My Family: Brian, who makes anything and everything possible, and is absolutely the best partner in life; Olivia, my brilliant co-pilot and muse; Conor & Donovan, my extraordinary and compassionate sons. I am in awe and so proud of you. Nanas & Papas, I love and appreciate you. **Keep Lighting Up The World.**

Momala: I have certainly risen higher by standing on your strong shoulders. Thank you for being my most important teacher. **Keep Hope Alive.**

My Book Advisors: This book was made possible by the unwavering encouragement and support of Brilliant Bookbound Founder Fran Hauser, Word Goddess Corrie Jackson, and Creative Genius Liliana Guia. **Keep Making Magic.**

My Mentees & Beta Readers: Jumana Attarwala, Ruth-Ann Bucknor, Jane Jiang, Molly Rochlin, Kiana White, Priya Natarajan, and Asija Qyteza. Thanks for sharing your Gen Z perspective. You are all rock stars! **Keep Shining.**

The Kick-Ass Women in my orbit who have inspired me, especially Ana Chadwick, Jen Ezring, Fran Hauser, Carla Harris, Cheyenne Tyler Jacobs, Mita Mallick, Karen McDonald, Fran Pastore, Amy Rochlin, Patti Russo, and Dr. Vida Samuel. **Keep Rising.**

The LiveGirl Board of Directors, Advisory Council, Staff, and Community: Thank you for working passionately and tirelessly to build a more equal, inclusive future. I am deeply grateful to LiveGirl's OG angel investors, including the Calhouns and the Cioffis, and all those who believe. **Keep Dreaming.**

Finally, to all of the young women out there ready to change the world: I see you. I hear you—your voice matters. ***Unleash Your Confidence and rise as a leader.***

Sheri West is a former Fortune 500 management executive turned social entrepreneur and the founder and CEO of women's leadership organization LiveGirl. She is a career-readiness expert, podcast host, and champion for equity and inclusion, with over 25 years of corporate and leadership development experience. West founded LiveGirl in 2014 to pay it forward to the next generation of diverse female leaders—and has served over 18,000 girls to date through its free-of-charge leadership development, mentorship, career readiness, and advocacy programs. West regularly speaks on women's leadership and career readiness, co-hosts the award-winning *Confident* podcast with her college daughter, and publishes the popular LinkedIn newsletter, *Confidence Unleashed*. She serves on various boards and loudly advocates for policies and practices that open doors for women and girls. In 2024, she was named one of the 100 Women to Know in America. Visit SheriWestLeadership.com.

For more leadership and career resources, scan the QR code.